D0898004

BOTTICELLI

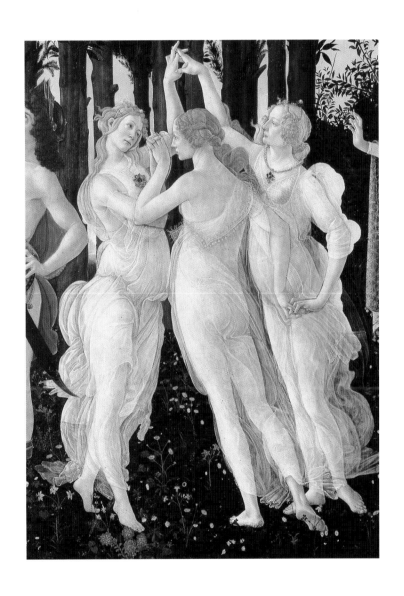

For Ron

Chaucer Press
20 Bloomsbury Street, London WC1B 3JH

© Chaucer Editions, 2004

ISBN 1904449 212

A copy of the CIP data is available from the
British Library upon request

Designed by Pointing Design Consultancy

This book, edited by Christopher Wright,
is a revised and updated version of an edition first published in 1979

Printed in China by Sun Fung Offset Binding Co. Ltd.

BOTTICELLI

Susan Legouix

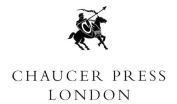

CHAUCER PRESS
LONDON

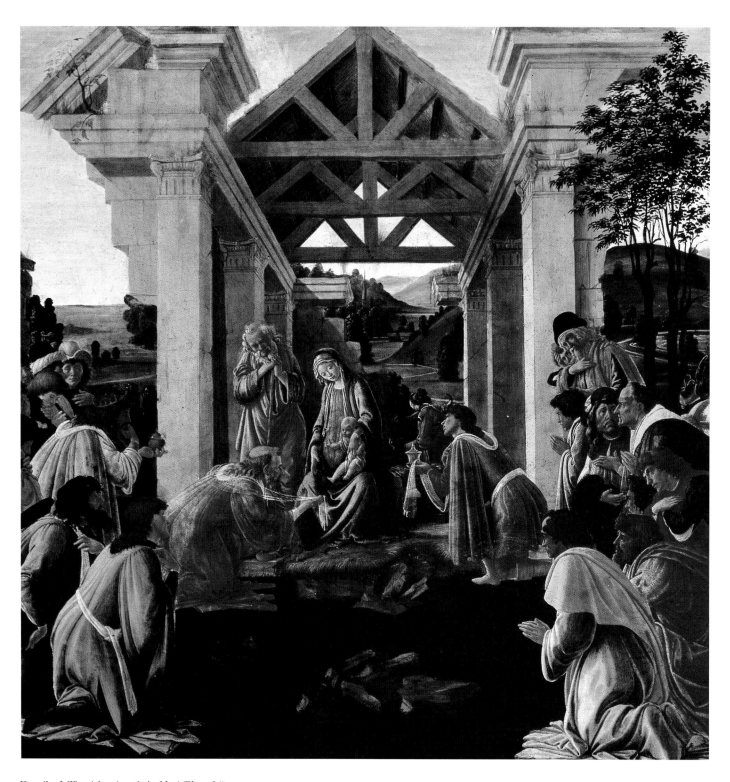

Detail of *The Adoration of the Magi* (Plate 24)

ACKNOWLEDGEMENTS

I am especially grateful to Allan Braham of the National Gallery for making the Eastlake notebooks available to me and for his useful comments on the portrait, formerly of the Merton collection, Peter Dreyer of the Staatliche Museen, Berlin; Christa Gardner; Martin Kemp of Glasgow University for generously allowing me to read his article on the Glasgow *Annunciation* prior to publication; Lady Merton for permission to reproduce the *Portrait of a Young Man Holding a Medallion*; Joyce Plesters of the National Gallery for information on Botticelli's technique and Christopher Wright for encouraging me to undertake the whole project.

Sincere thanks are also due to the following for their help in providing photographs and information: Accademia Carrara, Bergamo; Alte Pinakothek, Munich; Biblioteca Apostolica Vaticana, Vatican City; Bildarchiv Preussischer Kulturbesitz, Berlin; British Museum, London; Capilla Real, Granada; City Art Gallery, Birmingham; Church of Sant' Anna dei Lombardi, Naples; Church of Santa Maria Novella, Florence; Fratelli Alinari, Florence; Gabinetto Fotografico Nazionale, Rome; Galleria degli Uffizi, Florence; Gallerie Nazionale di Capodimonte, Naples; Galleria Pallavicini-Rospigliosi, Rome; Isabella Stewart Gardner Museum, Boston; Glasgow Art Gallery, Glasgow; Metropolitan Museum of Art, New York; Monastery of Ognissanti, Florence; Musée du Louvre, Paris; Museo del' Opera del Duomo, Florence; Museo del Prado, Madrid; Museo Poldi-Pezzoli, Milan; National Gallery, London; National Gallery of Art, Washington; National Gallery of Scotland, Edinburgh; Oronoz S.A., Madrid; Philadelphia Museum of Art, Philadelphia; Pinacoteca Ambrosiana, Milan; Service de Documentation Photographique de la Réunion des Musées Nationaux, Paris; Staatliche Gemäldegalerie, Berlin; Staatliche Gemäldegalerie, Dresden.

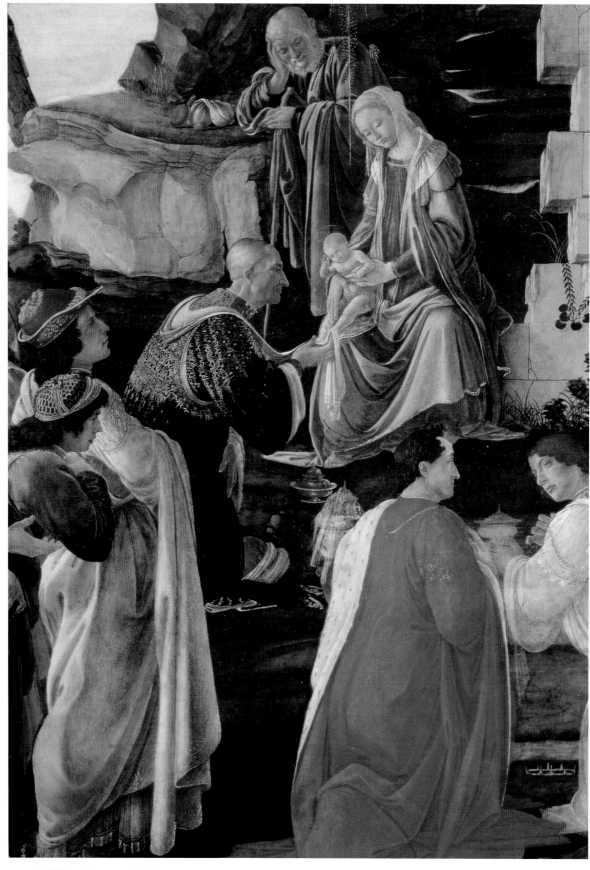

Detail of *The Adoration of the Magi* (Plate 22)

SANDRO BOTTICELLI

This book illustrates over sixty paintings by Botticelli. Only one, *The Mystic Nativity* (Plate 21), is signed and dated, and only one group, the Sistine Chapel frescoes (Plates 30–36,38), is still in its original position. We know almost nothing about the life and character of the artist, and there is an awkward period of almost ten years at the end of his life when, for reasons as yet unknown, he seems to have abandoned painting altogether.

Such an accumulation of negative factors might be a deterrent to further investigation were it not for the magic of the images which survive. Botticelli's art has proved more magnetic to historians and critics during the past hundred years than that of any other fifteenth-century painter. Over forty serious studies have found a place on library shelves, and almost half as many picture books occupy the coffee tables and bookcases of the art lovers of the world.

The very high survival rate of Botticelli's work compensates for the lack of documentation. Sixty or so paintings, a collection of drawings and many associated studio works is a surprisingly large *oeuvre* for such an early master, and it enables us to make an assessment of his style which is likely to be far better balanced than our view of the work of a painter such as the ill-fated Mantegna who is represented today by only a tiny proportion of his original output.

The city of Florence and the quality of life it offered in the fifteenth century made Botticelli's work what it is. Florence was his birthplace and the town where he spent the whole of his life apart from a short visit to Pisa in 1474 and about a year spent in Rome from 1481–82. The Ognissanti region of Florence, where his family the Filipepi were tanners, was the centre of the wool-working industry. The Vespucci, near neighbours of the Filipepi and patrons of Botticelli, were most important in their own time as dealers in wool and silk, but are best remembered for the fact that Amerigo, one of their sons, gave a name to the New World. Their house and the one that Botticelli occupied for most of his life were in the Via del Porcellana which runs between Borgo Ognissanti and Via Palazzuolo (see map, pages 24–25). Vasari recounted a story which if it can be relied upon gives us a rare glimpse of Botticelli's character, and even if it is not altogether true does illustrate vividly the hazards of living amidst the busy fabric industry. A cloth weaver moved eight looms into the house next door to Botticelli's and so disturbed the artist with the deafening sound and vibration of his machines that work became impossible. Gaining no favourable response from his polite request for a little peace and quiet, Botticelli was finally driven to take desperate retaliatory action. On a high wall at the side of his house he balanced an enormous stone in such a position that at any suggestion of vibration it threatened to crash through the weaver's roof. The result was, according to Vasari, that the neighbour was forced to mend his ways and come to an amicable agreement with Botticelli.

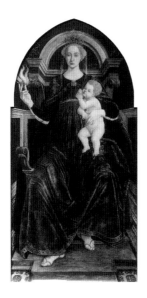

fig. 1 Antonio and Piero POLLAIVOLO *Charity*
Florence, Galleria degli Uffizi. Tempera on panel.

The Pollaiuolo brothers were responsible for paintings of the six Virtues, Faith, Hope, Charity, Temperence, Prudence and Justice, and Botticelli for the seventh, Fortitude, for the hall of the Arte della Mercanzia in Florence. It is generally believed that Piero Pollaiuolo painted *Charity* and the other panels, but scholars also believe that his brother Antonio had a hand in the designs of the figures. A comparison between this picture and Botticelli's *Fortitude* (Plate 6) shows how Botticelli imitated certain elements of the Pollaiuolo stylistic language, in particular the mannered treatment of hands and feet. Botticelli's figure, however, sits much more naturally on her throne than the *Charity* or any of the other *Virtues*.

Artists' workshops were themselves 'home industries' and by 1472 when Botticelli's name first appeared in the record books of the painters' guild he already had an assistant, the fifteen- or sixteen-year-old Filippino Lippi, son of Filippo Lippi who had died a few years earlier in 1469. By 1480 Botticelli's studio was firmly established and in a legal declaration of that year he listed three assistants, Raffaello di Lorenzo di Frosino Tosi, Giovanni di Benedetto Gianfanini and Jacopo di Domenico Papi. Elsewhere assistants named Jacopo, Biagio and Ludovico are mentioned, but the only one to emerge as an artist of individual talent was Filippino Lippi. Botticelli's own training in the 1460s appears to have taken place in the studio of Filippino's father Filippo Lippi. Certain features of his earliest pictures such as the architectural setting of the *Madonna and Child in an Archway* (Plate 2) and the *Madonna and Child with Two Angels* (Plate 3) can be seen to have been directly derived from models by Lippi, and Botticelli's sweet-faced women, so effusively praised in the literature of the early part of the twentieth century, are the natural descendants of Lippi's Madonnas and female saints.

In addition to Lippi the artists who made the most impression on the young painter were the Pollaiuolo brothers (fig. 1), with whom he worked in the hall of the Arte della Mercanzia (see Plate 6), and Verrocchio, the master of Leonardo. The influence of Verrocchio is most apparent in the early Madonna and Child pictures, such as those in the Uffizi (Plates 1 and 2), Naples (Plate 3) and Boston (Plate 4). These Madonnas wear robes and headdresses very similar to those of Verrocchio's Madonnas in the *Madonna and Child* in the Staatliche Gemäldegaleric, Berlin (Dahlem) (fig. 2), and *The Ruskin Madonna*, now in the National Gallery of Scotland, Edinburgh (fig. 3). The facial features of the Madonnas in these pictures by Verrocchio and Botticelli are also strikingly alike. The relationship with Antonio and Piero Pollaiuolo is discernible mainly in the drawing of male figures and in the articulation of the limbs of figures in movement (fig. 4). The sinuous form of Holofernes in *The Finding of the Dead Holofernes* (Plate 56), which was probably painted around 1470, the period of the decorations in the hall of the Arte della Mercanzia, is reminiscent of nudes by Antonio Pollaiuolo, but by the time Botticelli painted the reclining Mars in *Venus and Mars* (Plate 62) in the late 1480s, the influence was no longer

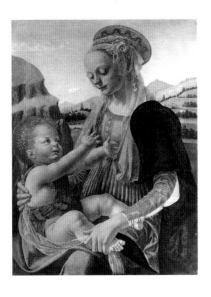

fig. 2 Andrea del VERROCCHIO
Madonna and Child Berlin Gemäldegalerie.
Tempera on panel.

The Madonna in this picture and *The Ruskin Madonna* (fig. 3) are clearly related to early pictures by Botticelli such as the *Madonna and Child in an Archway* (Plate 2) and the *Madonna and Child with Symbols of the Eucharist.* (Plate 4).

important. Similarities with Verrocchio also cease to be noticeable in the pictures of the 1480s although the pretty, feminine spirit of Lippi lingered and played a part in Botticelli's style until his latest period of the 1490s.

Filippo Lippi was lucky enough to be one of the generation of artists befriended and patronized by Cosimo 'il Vecchio' de' Medici, and Botticelli had equal good fortune in that his coming of age as a painter coincided with the assumption of Cosimo's grandson, Lorenzo 'il Magnifico', to the leadership of the Medici family and its party on the death of his father, Piero 'the Gouty', in 1469. It is not known precisely how much work Botticelli executed for the Palazzo Medici in Florence, but an inventory made at the time of Lorenzo's death in 1492 records a *Fortuna* and a standard decorated with a *Pallas* made for a famous tournament organized by the Medici in the Piazza Santa Croce in 1475. In addition, Vasari mentioned portraits of Lucrezia Tornabuoni, mother of Lorenzo de' Medici, and of Simonetta Vespucci and a *Bacchus*, all hanging in various parts of the Palazzo Medici. Like the decorative frescoes painted for the Medici family at their country villas of Spedaletto, near Volterra, and Castello, just outside Florence, these works are all lost. Happily three major paintings commissioned by Lorenzo's second cousin Lorenzo di Pierfrancesco de' Medici do survive, *Pallas and the Centaur* (Plate 65), *Primavera* (Plate 67) and *The Birth of Venus* (Plate 68). All three are believed to have been executed for the Villa di Castello. They were only removed from there and seen for the first time by the public in the nineteenth century. Botticelli's relationship with Lorenzo di Pierfrancesco appears to have been very close. In 1496 when the Medici administration was on the point of collapse and any written communication to the family was in danger of being intercepted by political opponents, Michelangelo despatched a letter to Lorenzo di Pierfrancesco addressed to 'Sandro di bottjcello in firenze'. The trust between this member of the Medici family and Botticelli was of particular importance as it gave the artist the freedom he required to produce his most original and extraordinary work, the illustrated *Divina Commedia* (Plates 71–74).

Although the two pictures most familiar today, *Primavera* and *The Birth of Venus*, were Medici commissions, most of Botticelli's time and energy was devoted to working for the Church, as can be

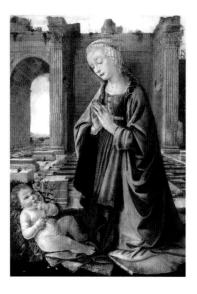

fig. 3 Andrea del VERROCCHIO
Madonna and Child (The Ruskin Madonna)
Edinburgh, National Gallery of Scotland.
Tempera transferred from panel to canvas.

Although this picture is very closely related to other Madonna
and Child groups attributed to Verrocchio, it has also been
proposed that it might be an early work of Leonardo da Vinci
executed in Verrocchio's workshop.

seen from a glance at the map of Florence on pages 24–25 illustrating the original distribution of the
pictures in the city. As Botticelli undertook no multiple-panel altar pieces there are practically no
reconstructions of altar pieces or fresco cycles to be made and historians have tended to pay little
attention to the sites in Florence for which many of the pictures were painted, though on occasions they
may have a bearing on the final appearance of the work. The Berlin *St Sebastian* (Plate 7) is an interesting
case. It hung originally, we are told, 'in una colonna' in the Church of Santa Maria Maggiore, and the
deduction that the picture is tall and narrow because it hung on a pillar, though fundamental, is only one
of the conclusions which follows. Santa Maria Maggiore is a three-aisled hall, one of the oldest
churches in Florence, supported by solid quadrangular piers which measure 87.5 cm. in width at eye
level. The first column on the right is frescoed with two tiers of full-length saints, probably executed by
two or more different fourteenth-century artists. The lower tier of the east face of this pier is occupied
by an *Execution of St Sebastian*. Since representations of archers as well as of the saint himself had to be
fitted into the limited space, the individual figure of St Sebastian is half the size of the other seven
saints decorating this column. The composition is crowded and uncomfortably out of scale with the
other figures, and it is quite feasible that Botticelli's own recognition of the shortcomings of this earlier
painting led him to make his *St Sebastian* for the same church a single figure composition. It is even
possible that Botticelli's panel was made to hang over the fresco, but as yet no record has been found of
who commissioned his painting.

The Bardi Altarpiece (Plate 9) of 1485, now in Berlin, is another picture which may have been
influenced by the nature of its original location. It occupied the first altar on the left on the back wall of
the chancel in Santo Spirito. There is not a great deal of evidence that Botticelli was an artist particularly
sensitive to the fall of light, but the direction of the light source in the Bardi Chapel does coincide with
that in the picture. What may be more significant is the architecture, or lack of architecture, in the
composition. Brunelleschi's Santo Spirito was one of the great new churches of Florence, a model for
architects of Botticelli's generation. Rather than compete with Brunelleschi and place his figures in their

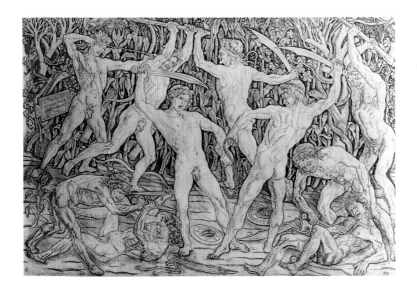

fig. 4 Antonio POLLAIUOLO
Battle of Nude Men
London, Victoria and Albert
Museum (Department of Prints
and Drawings). Engraving.

Although Botticelli's early
development reflected the
influence of Pollaiuolo the nudes
in this 'battle' illustrate an
obsessive interest in dynamic
movement which is very different
from the grace of, for instance,
Botticelli's *St Sebastian* (Plate 7).

own architectural setting, as did, for example, Cosimo Roselli in his *Madonna Enthroned* of 1482 nearby in the transept, Botticelli constructed rich leafy arches which serve the function of architecture in framing and setting off the figures, but which bear no relation to any building style. There is every indication that the picture is one of the most painstakingly composed and executed of the artist's works and so it is not altogether surprising to learn that the frame, now lost, was made by Giuliano da Sangallo, the eminent architect who only a few years later was working on the fabric of Santo Spirito, building the sacristy. A tondo still furnished with an original frame, *The Virgin and Child with St John and an Angel* (fig. 5) in London, is inscribed on the back [*M?*] *Giuljano da san Ghallo*, which may signify another case of collaboration between the two artists.

For making the frame of *The Bardi Altarpiece* Sangallo received almost a third as much as Botticelli was paid for painting the picture. But these figures are misleading unless examined in more detail. Of Botticelli's seventy-eight florins, thirty-eight were for the gold and gilding of the altarpiece, and of Sangallo's twenty-four florins a fair proportion must have been spent on materials. What emerges from the figures is the high price paid for embellishments. Of a total of 102 florins paid by Agnolo Bardi for the altarpiece only thirty-five florins went towards the artist's brushwork. The picture would not of course have been the same without the embellishments. The decorative character of Botticelli's art has always been recognized as one of its greatest qualities, though in the twentieth century a preoccupation with iconographical questions tended to override considerations of the glory of ornamentation. The astute Herbert Horne, whose monograph on Botticelli is an essential point of departure for all later studies, observed that in nineteenth-century England 'The pictures of Botticelli and his school, like those of Crivelli, were sought out for their decorative beauty before their finer and more artistic traits had been duly appreciated, or even realised.'

Horne's coupling of the names of Botticelli and Crivelli is not merely fortuitous. Subconsciously he pinpointed a deeper truth about the place of Botticelli in history. In an age when we are conditioned to search for historical and artistic developments, it is disturbingly difficult to accommodate neatly the

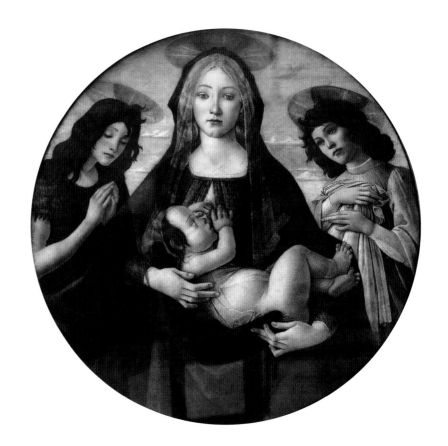

fig. 5 Studio of BOTTICELLI
*The Virgin and Child with St John
and an Angel* London, National
Gallery. Tempera on panel.
Original frame.

Although this is generally
acknowledged today to be a
studio piece it is a most appealing
picture, competently executed.
Similar shiny haloes appear in a
*Madonna and Child Embraced by St
John* in the Pitti Palace, Florence,
which may be by the same hand.

work of Crivelli and Botticelli. Both occupy their own private culs-de-sac. By the end of Crivelli's life Titian was almost ten years old and by Botticelli's death in 1510 Raphael was working on the Stanze of the Vatican and Michelangelo on the ceiling of the Sistine Chapel. If few pictures survived by Crivelli or Botticelli we could be forgiven for imagining that Crivelli might have worked towards a style which looked finally something like that of the early Titian, and that Botticelli's late work looked rather Raphaelesque. Yet the reality is that if any of Botticelli's work looks remotely Raphaelesque it is that of his middle rather than of his late period, and that the passage of time sees his art and that of Crivelli move into a distinctly Gothic idiom.

If it is true of any artist it is true of Botticelli that his art was a personal statement. It can be enjoyed for its own sake regardless of its place in any pattern of development which historians with hindsight project as to the period and style to which it belongs. Yet doggedly we pursue the quest for a wider significance, with varying degrees of success depending on our interpretive skills. Wölfflin, whose particular objective was 'classic' art, wrote: 'He [Botticelli] succeeds in imparting this flowing line to his large masses, and where he orders his picture in a unified composition around one centre something specifically new is created, the consequences of which are of great importance. It is in this sense that his compositions of *The Adoration of the Magi* are to be considered.' It may not be especially helpful to seek

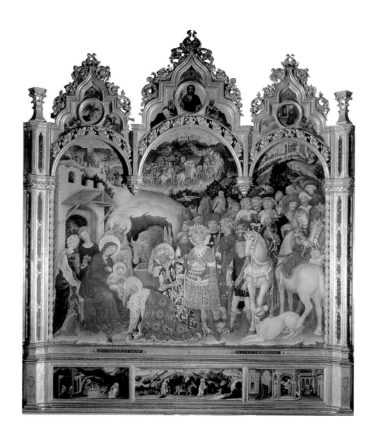

fig. 6 Gentile da FABRIANO
The Adoration of the Magi Florence,
Galleria degli Uffizi.
Tempera on panel.

This glorious altarpiece would have
been seen by Botticelli in the Strozzi
Chapel in Santa Trinità, Florence,
where it originally hung.

out these 'consequences', but an examination and comparison of the five surviving Adoration and
Nativity pictures does reveal many of the nuances of Botticelli's personal style over the thirty-year
period of his working life. Visitors to London are fortunate enough to be able to see three of these five
pictures hanging in the National Gallery. The remaining two are in the Uffizi, Florence, and the
National Gallery of Art, Washington.

The earliest of the Adorations is the small but wide panel in London (Plate 17). The Virgin and Child
are placed to one side of the picture and a huge crowd of figures led by the Magi stream away from
them. The scheme is much the same as that used by Gentile da Fabriano as early as 1423 in his famous
Adoration of the Magi now in the Uffizi (fig. 6). Like Gentile, Botticelli made his first king kneel to kiss the
toe of Christ and the second kneel and remove his crown. The figure style adopted by Botticelli in the
picture is very close to that of Lippi, so close that many scholars agree with Horne that this is 'one very
early painting' by the artist, probably done soon after he left his master's studio. The highly experimental
nature of the technique, apparent in the numerous revisions of certain areas of *The Adoration*, and the
struggle which has gone into the depiction of the architecture are additional signs of immaturity, but
the picture could not be called incompetent. The characterization of the figures is remarkably varied
and expressive. Two young shepherds who make a speedy entry on the right are related to a pair who

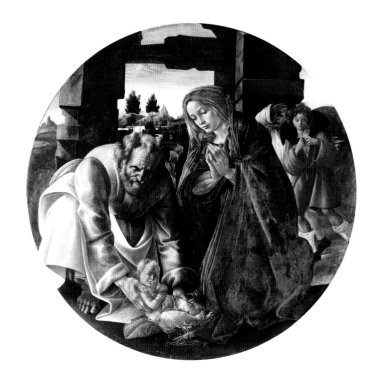

fig. 7 Studio of BOTTICELLI
The Holy Family Boston, Isabella Stewart
Gardner Museum. Tempera on panel.

This picture is composed of a curious
patchwork of styles, and it has even been
suggested that the massive St Joseph is the
work of the young Michelangelo.

appear with rather less verve in a much later studio picture in the Isabella Stewart Gardner Museum, Boston (fig. 7). Their origin is mysterious. Mantegna introduced a similar but more uncouth pair on the right-hand side of his *Adoration of the Shepherds* of about 1450 in the Metropolitan Museum, New York (fig. 8), as did Antonio Rosellino in his relief *Nativity* in Naples (fig. 9) of the 1470s.

The tondo *Adoration of the Magi* in London (Plate 19) repeats a number of the figures from the first picture, such as the man to the extreme left who blows his nose, but it is certainly a work of greater maturity. The success of the composition can only be fully realized if it is placed against an earlier circular Adoration such as that by Filippo Lippi in the National Gallery of Art, Washington (fig. 10). Whereas Lippi simply condensed the traditional rectangular grouping, Botticelli moved the Virgin right back into the centre of the circle and allowed her to be smaller than the foreground members of the crowd. Attention is skillfully focused on her by the grouping of the surrounding figures and by the arrangement of the monumental ruined architecture which soars above.

The figures in the third *Adoration of the Magi* (Plate 22) in the Uffizi are much larger in scale than those in the two London pictures, but even so they must have been dwarfed by the vast interior of Santa Maria Novella where the picture originally was. Vasari called it 'a truly admirable work, executed so beautifully, in colouring, drawing, and composition, that every craftsman today marvels at it'. He pointed out that most of the figures in the picture are portraits of the Medici family and their entourage. It must have been the call for portraits in the commission, in addition to the size of the church, which dictated the scale of the figures. In order to represent each person as clearly as possible Botticelli not only made each larger than his counter-part in the London pictures, but he also placed the group on a slight slope so that the heads could be seen above each other. This picture was painted around 1475–77, perhaps only five or six years after the London tondo. The increase of naturalism in Botticelli's style during this period can be demonstrated by a comparison of the horse's head on the left

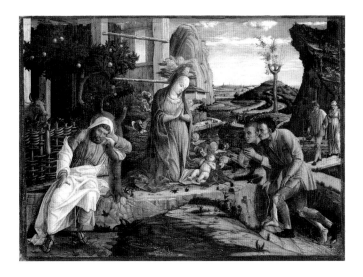

fig. 8 Andrea MANTEGNA
The Adoration of the Shepherds
New York, Metropolitan Museum of Art.
Tempera transferred from panel to canvas.

of the composition (Plate 22) with horses in the London pictures. Instead of being a formalized creature apparently drawn from Antique sculpture, the horse in the Uffizi *Adoration* is a tactile quivering beast who nuzzles at the arm of his owner. The Madonna presenting her child to the oldest king, a portrait of Cosimo de' Medici, differs very little from the earlier representations of her. Her curiously extended torso suggests that Botticelli might have used sculptural models such as Donatello's *St John* (fig. 11) for studies of seated figures. It is usually supposed that the *St John* was deliberately made very tall so that in his original position on the façade of the Duomo the figure appeared in proportion when seen from the ground. But Donatello surely over-compensated, for the *St John* sat in the lowest row of niches, and if an artist were to place himself at a comfortable distance to draw the sculpture he would have seen a figure with an exaggeratedly tall body and short legs, rather like Botticelli's seated Madonnas.

Vasari said of the Uffizi *Adoration* that it brought Botticelli considerable fame, both in Florence and further afield and led to the call to Rome to work in the Sistine Chapel. The fourth of the known Adoration pictures, the one now in Washington (Plate 24), is thought to have been executed in Rome and it represents a turning point in Botticelli's approach to the subject and perhaps in his whole career. It is in many respects the least 'Botticellian' and the most classical of his Adorations. Significantly, it is probably the picture Wölfflin had in mind when he spoke of Botticelli's creation of 'a unified composition around one centre'. Critics have often commented that the picture shows the influence of Perugino and Signorelli whom Botticelli met while working in the Sistine Chapel. The influence could have been through one specific composition, *The Nativity* fresco by Perugino which, until Michelangelo obliterated it with his *Last Judgement*, occupied the right-hand side of the altar wall of the chapel (see diagram, p. 68). It is unlikely that Signorelli arrived in Rome until after Botticelli and the other artists left, so the suggestion of his influence can be safely discounted. There is unfortunately no record of the appearance of Perugino's composition, but it could easily have been set in a landscape similar to the one

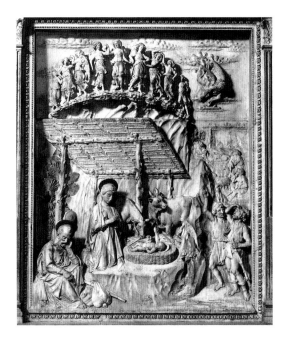

fig. 9 Antonio ROSELLINO
The Nativity
Naples, Church of Sant' Anna dei Lombardi.
Marble relief.

Antonio Rosellino carved this relief in the
1470s as the altarpiece for the tomb chapel of
Maria of Aragón in the Church of Sant' Anna
dei Lombardi. The work was carried out in
Florence and then transported to Naples. It has
been suggested that the shepherds could have
been influenced by Hugo van der Goes's
Portinari Altarpiece, but it is now known that this
did not arrive in Florence until 1483, after
Rosellino's death.

in Botticelli's picture and it might have had a 'stable' with a heavy king-post roof on a row of sharply
receding columns like the one in the Washington *Adoration*. Features of architecture and landscape
related to this *Adoration* occur in other pictures by Perugino.

Botticelli's classical 'Peruginesque' period lasted throughout the 1480s and probably culminated in
The Coronation of the Virgin (Plate 15), after which the very personal style of the *Divina Commedia*
illustrations (Plates 71–74) and *The Mystic Nativity* (Plate 21) gradually emerged. Although not illustrated
in this book because of their damaged and incomplete state, there exist fragments of two further
Adoration of the Magi pictures which appear to be developments of the Washington composition and
which are in the possession of the Soprintendenza alle Gallerie, Florence, the Pierpont Morgan Library,
New York and the Fitzwilliam Museum, Cambridge, the last two being elements of one picture.

If it were possible to hang the Washington *Adoration of the Magi* next to the London *Mystic Nativity*
viewers unfamiliar with the work of Botticelli might justifiably find it hard to believe that both pictures
were by the same hand. The artist's latest style is most perfectly exemplified in *The Mystic Nativity* of
1500–01. The following passage was written by John Addington Symonds about Fra Angelico, but it
translates into words a spirit so close to that of the late Botticelli, and *The Mystic Nativity* in particular,
that I quote it in full: 'His world is a strange one – a world not of hills and fields and flowers and men of
flesh and blood, but one where people are embodied ecstasies, the colours tints from evening clouds or
apocalyptic jewels, the scenery a flood of light or a background of illuminated gold. His mystic gardens,
where ransomed souls embrace, and dance with angels on the lawns outside the City of the Lamb, are
such as were never trodden by the foot of man in any paradise of earth.' Botticelli may have been
remembering Fra Angelico's *Last Judgement* in San Marco when he drew the foreground figures in *The
Mystic Nativity*, and the dancing angels in the sky recall those in Rosellino's *Nativity* (fig. 9) but the style of
the painting is outside most fifteenth-century terms of reference. He returned to the Gothic principle

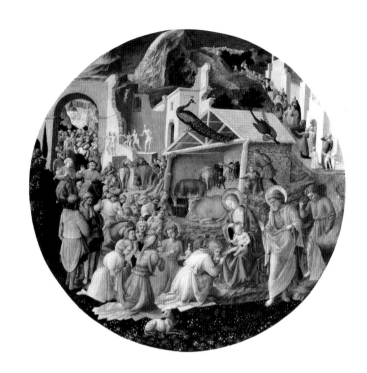

fig. 10 Filippo LIPPI
The Adoration of the Magi
Washington, National Gallery of Art (Samuel
H. Kress collection). Tempera on panel.

This picture of about 1445 is an early, if not
the earliest, tondo Adoration composition. It
is thought to have been conceived and
perhaps partially executed by Fra Angelico and
completed by Filippo Lippi. It is not known
where in Florence it originally hung.

whereby the most important character in a composition was the largest in scale, and he abandoned modern architecture and scientific perspective in favour of a rural setting in which natural rock appears to have erupted from the shifting earth's crust in order to frame and protect the Holy Family. In many ways the picture is a synthesis of old and new in Botticelli's art. It is archaic in iconography and in the extensive use of gold, which underlies the whole of the thatch roof, the upper part of the sky and the dancing angels, but it is new in that it appears to have been executed in oil on canvas rather than Botticelli's usual tempera on panel, and in that it seems likely that it was painted purely as a vehicle for self-expression. The concept of 'art for art's sake' is more often associated with the sixteenth century and the Mannerist movement than with the late quattrocento, but the fact that *The Mystic Nativity* so unashamedly fails to meet the requirements of spatial realism and naturalism of an up-to-date picture of 1500 almost certainly precludes it from being a commission for public view.

A poignantly beautiful picture which is stylistically very close to *The Mystic Nativity* is the Granada *Agony in the Garden* (Plate 25), which was a commission but was destined for a site well away from the Florentine avant-garde. The composition differs little in essentials from an anonymous woodcut illustration of the same subject (fig. 12) made at least half a century earlier. Again Botticelli found the style of an earlier period more appropriate to his expressive need than that of his own time.

Also closely akin to *The Mystic Nativity* in its non-realistic approach is the illustrated *Divina Commedia* (Plates 71–74). Herbert Read in *The Art of Sculpture* wrote: 'The theory of perspective developed in the fifteenth century is a scientific convention; it is merely one way of describing space and has no absolute validity'. Botticelli treated the theory as if it had no validity whatsoever in the Dante drawings. Through the cantos of the *Inferno, Purgatorio* and *Paradiso* he turned art and the world upside down. In episode after episode fierce curling flames pour out of the ground and sometimes out of half-open tilted rhomboid tombs, and figures gnaw at each others' and their own flesh in a world of sharp-edged rocks,

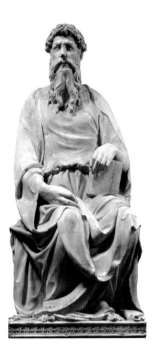

fig. 11 DONATELLO
St John the Evangelist
Florence, Museo del' Opera del Duomo. Marble.

A drawing by a Florentine artist of the second half of the sixteenth century in the Museo del' Opera del Duomo shows sculptures of the four Evangelists flanking the great west door of Florence Cathedral. Donatello's *St John* was on the right-hand side nearest the door.

deep caverns and vicious thorny woods. Gradually, the scenes become calmer and emptier of figures, and Dante is transported into a state of purity and joy which is *Paradiso*.

The intensity of these drawings and the latest paintings is often associated with the puritanizing cult of Fra Girolamo Savonarola of San Marco whose emotional rallying sermons finally led to political revolution and his own execution in Florence in 1498. It is not entirely clear how closely Botticelli was involved with the monk's near-hysterical form of religion. Vasari claims he became so ardent a follower that he gave up working and spent his last years in poverty and distress, but one of the few surviving documents concerning Botticelli's old age does not endorse this view. In 1502 the agent of the great patron of the arts Isabella d'Este, Marchioness of Mantua, a demanding lady who did not take kindly to emotional or capricious artists, wrote to his employer, 'Botticelli has been much extolled to me both as an excellent painter and as a man who works willingly . . .' This, written four years after Savonarola's death, does not seem like a description of a man whose head was turned by extremist religious fervour. Two years later Botticelli was one of the committee chosen to decide on a site for Michelangelo's *David*, which again indicates that he must still have been regarded as a man of stature in Florentine society.

One of the great qualities of Botticelli's *Divina Commedia* illustrations is the clarity of the narrative. As the scenes flow from page to page the forms of Dante and Virgil can always be easily identified and their gestures and expressions quickly interpreted. The experience of working in the Sistine Chapel (Plates 31–36, 38), where Botticelli had the more difficult task of being one of an artistic team creating a continuous theme, must have sharpened his sense of narrative. Some of his compositional arrangements in the Sistine frescoes were indeed more successful in this respect than those of other painters working in the chapel who, unlike Botticelli, had had the advantage of previous practice of fresco cycle painting. Agostino Taja's mid-eighteenth-century guide to the Vatican singled out Botticelli's *Punishment of the Rebels* (Plate 36) as being especially praiseworthy. In this painting, more than

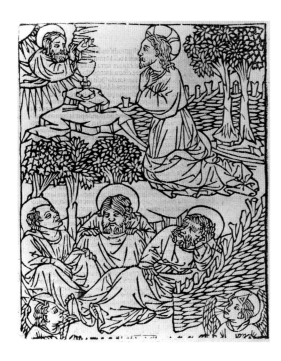

fig. 12 Venetian, c. 1450
The Agony in the Garden
New York, Metropolitan Museum of Art
(Harris Brisbane Dick fund). Woodcut.

This is one of the scenes from Bonaventura's *Meditatione sopra la Passione*, printed in 1487, which re-used illustrations from the Venetian block-book, *Passion of Our Lord*, of c. 1450.

in the other two which Botticelli painted for the Sistine Chapel, the background and surrounding architecture were manipulated to organize and punctuate the narrative. A centrally-placed arch is not an unusual feature in fifteenth-century compositions, Gozzoli used one in his *Jacob and Esau* which Botticelli could have seen in the Camposanto at Pisa, but its effectiveness in *The Punishment of the Rebels* is striking and may have inspired Ghirlandaio, one of the Sistine artists, when he painted his *Massacre of the Innocents* (fig. 13) in Santa Maria Novella.

Narrative is again the keynote of one of Botticelli's small mythological paintings, *The 'Calumny' of Apelles* (Plate 66) now in the Uffizi. The picture is literally composed from two or more written descriptions of the *Calumny* painted in the fourth century B.C. by the Greek artist Apelles. Perhaps with this picture subconsciously in his mind, Ruskin called Botticelli a 'reanimate Greek', and even before *The 'Calumny' of Apelles* had been painted a writer contemporary with Botticelli, Ugolino Verino, had called him 'the successor of Apelles'. Botticelli's connection with the Antique was usually less direct than in *The 'Calumny' of Apelles* and is generally far less easily understood. Although the majority of scholars now agree on the identification of the principal allegorical figures in *The Birth of Venus* (Plate 68) and the *Primavera* (Plate 67), neither picture illustrates an existing text as closely as *The 'Calumny'* follows Lucian's and Alberti's description of Apelles's painting.

The mythological pictures are set apart from the Christian Adorations, Annunciations and Madonnas as a result of the complexity and unfamiliarity of their subject matter and because they reveal Botticelli as a compositional innovator. Visual models for classical themes were few and far between in the quattrocento. Botticelli's solution was to adapt and transform suitable existing images with such skill and artistry that he appears to have created something absolutely new. No obvious model for *Venus and Mars* (Plate 62) can be found in panel painting of the period, but lovers are sometimes depicted reclining opposite each other in small scale decorative and engraved works of art, and a seemingly insignificant

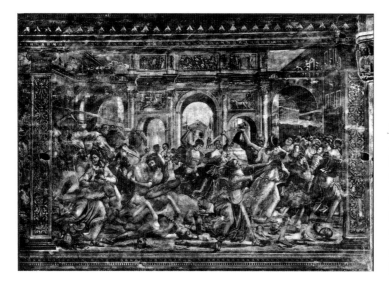

fig. 13 Domenico GHIRLANDAIO
The Massacre of the Innocents
Florence, Church of Santa Maria
Novella. Fresco.

Ghirlandaio worked beside Botticelli
in Ognissanti and in the Sistine Chapel
in Rome. His fresco cycle in the choir
of Santa Maria Novella was completed
in 1490.

detail such as the border of Baccio Baldini's *Pair of Dancers* (fig. 14) could have been the sort of image which provided the foundation for Botticelli's composition. It is possible that some Flemish tapestry may have inspired the strongly two-dimensional structure of the *Primavera* and, as Gombrich has suggested, the traditional arrangement of the Baptism of Christ may be the origin of the composition of his *Birth of Venus*.

The three Graces of the *Primavera* are loosely based on a classical sculpture group, such as one in the Libreria Piccolomini, Siena, but unlike the classical sculptor, and also unlike Raphael later on, Botticelli chose to make his Graces move. They are usually said to be dancing, but it might equally be said that their bodies are simply infused with a spirit of movement. Botticelli was not, as was Leonardo, interested in dynamics, and he introduced movement as a means of creating flowing linear compositions or as an expression of narrative content, but never in the interest of depicting the muscularity of the human body in action. Botticelli's figures are incapable of ever being entirely static. This is demonstrated by the comparison of one of Botticelli's 'still' figures, the St John the Baptist of *The Bardi Altarpiece* (Plate 9), with an earlier monumental depiction of the same saint in the same attitude by Domenico Veneziano (fig. 15).

We know from the composition of *The 'Calumny' of Apelles* that Botticelli had read Alberti's *De Pictura*. This treatise also contains some advice on movement which is graphically reflected in the *Primavera* and *The Birth of Venus*: 'it will be a good idea, when we wish clothing to have movement, to have in the corner of the picture the face of the West or South wind blowing between clouds and moving all the clothing before it. The pleasing result will be that those sides of the bodies the wind strikes will appear under the covering of the clothes almost as if they were naked, since the clothes are made to adhere to the body by the force of the wind . . .' On hair Alberti wrote, 'let it twist around as if to tie itself in a knot, and wave upwards in the air like flames, let it weave beneath other hair and

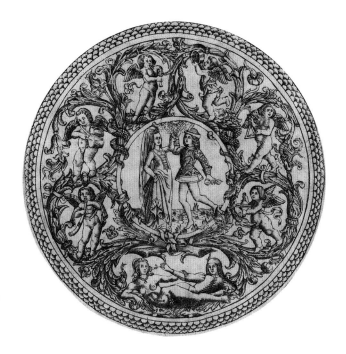

fig. 14 Baccio BALDINI
Pair of Dancers in a Wreath with Cupids London,
British Museum, Department of Prints and
Drawings. Engraving.

Vasari recounted that Baccio Baldini was the
engraver of Botticelli's designs for the 1481
edition of *La Divina Commedia* (Plates 71–74).
This *Pair of Dancers* of c. 1475 is one of the 'Otto
Prints', a series of hunting and amorous scenes
intended to be pasted into gift boxes.

sometimes lift on one side and another'. The hair of Venus in *The Birth of Venus* was created almost as if by Alberti's command.

Although the words of Alberti on movement fit Botticelli's images so well that we cannot fail to associate the two, the artist never allowed himself to be bound by rules. Unpredictability is a characteristic of his art. In *La Divina Commedia, Inferno*, Canto XXXII Botticelli drew Dante with two heads in order to express the turning movement which follows the shifting of the poet's attention from one subject to another. The lack of respect for accepted artistic convention which Botticelli displayed on occasion can easily confuse the historian whose job it is to unravel the meaning of the images. The two-headed Dante is unlikely to be misunderstood in the context of a series, but in the large mythological paintings, which have no continuous narrative content, the borderline between what is meant to be pure representation and what is 'artistic licence' is more subtle. In *The Birth of Venus* the two figures flying in from the left propelling Venus towards the shore are usually taken to be zephyrs, but the author of a fairly recent reappraisal of the picture calls the female figure Chloris, the earth nymph, because in his opinion she is not blowing and has no wings. In fact it is clear from the original picture that a stream of breath or wind is issuing from her lips and she *does* have wings. There are four wings behind the entwined figures, and although the two wings behind the woman do not appear to be attached to her anatomically correctly, why should something that is in essence 'unreal', as figures do not have wings, be painted in a 'real' way? Botticelli no doubt felt that it was quite sufficient to state that four wings shared out between two people meant two wings each. This kind of visual shorthand is carried right through *The Birth of Venus*. The waves from which Venus has risen are, as Yashiro, the most inspired of Botticelli's biographers, observed, 'as unreal as they can be'. They appear as a pattern of white 'V' shapes on a flat ground of light greenish-blue which makes little attempt to suggest the transparency and wetness of water. The tree trunks too, on the right, are stiff brown columns which are

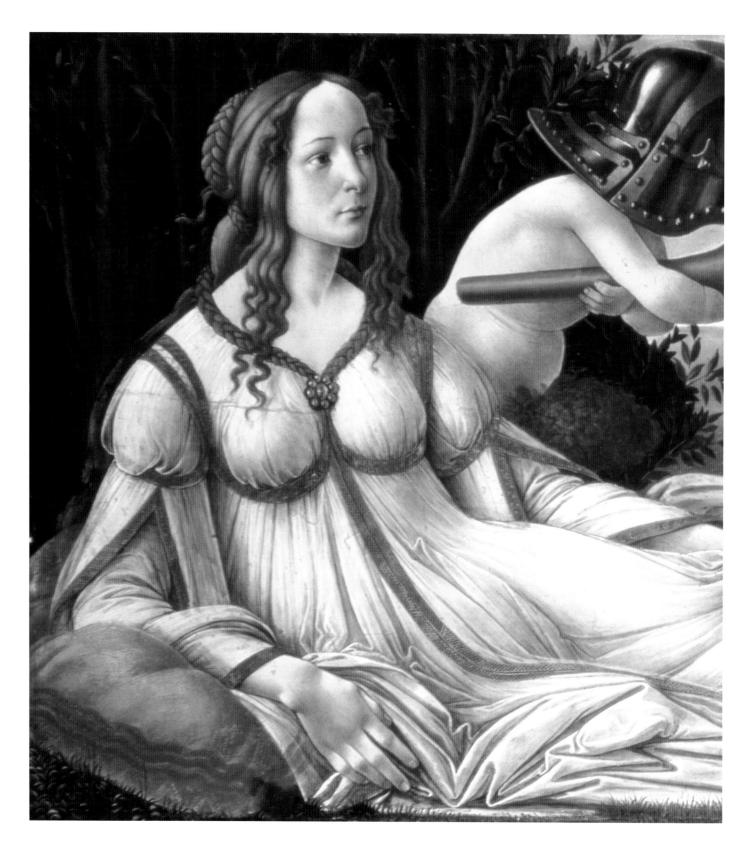

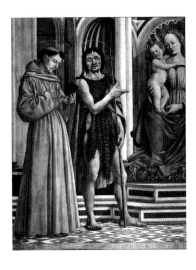

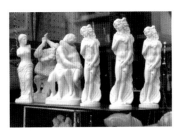

fig. 16 Miniature figures of Botticelli's *Venus*, cast in alabaster powder or some other compound, are found not only in Italian gift shops. In a shop in Kent they jostle with Rodin's *The Kiss* and the *Venus de Milo*.

fig. 15 Domenico VENEZIANO
Madonna and Child with Saints, detail of St John
Florence, Galleria degli Uffizi. Tempera on panel.

The picture was painted for the Church of Santa Lucia de' Magnoli in Florence in the mid-1440s. It is often referred to as *The St Lucy Altarpiece*.

more akin to architecture than to nature, and their unreality is heightened, as if that were necessary, by a strip of gold applied in short regular strokes down one side of each trunk.

The combination of esoteric subject matter and bold and fluent design which caused certain nineteenth-century authors to shy away from *The Birth of Venus* also made the picture, conversely, one of the most popular images in Italian art in the twentieth century. In Crowe and Cavalcaselle's *History of Italian Painting* (1911) the only comment on the style of the painting is 'The figures are a little out of balance'. Today the figure of Venus in particular is so well loved that it has even been translated into three-dimensional form for mass sale in Britain and abroad (fig. 16) and is so familiar that a large proportion of the viewers of BBC television's *Monty Python's Flying Circus* could be expected to recognize her when, seen on the screen as a cut-out with articulated legs, she performed a variation of the Charleston on the edge of her shell. *The Birth of Venus* above all other of Botticelli's paintings has 'stage presence'. Kenneth Clark recalls its dramatic entrance to the famous 1930 exhibition of Italian art at Burlington House, London. 'With my love of *coups de théâtre* I asked the Academy attendants to keep Botticelli's *Birth of Venus* on one side until I could collect everyone working on the hanging to watch her rise from the basement into the gallery; and it was an unforgettable moment.' Lord Clark had seen the picture many times before, but viewing it in different surroundings and, literally, from an unusual angle, he experienced its impact anew. For those of us who have to make a fresh presentation of Botticelli's pictures in words and photographs alone the task is more difficult. We can only ask, as Walter Pater did in 1870, 'What is the peculiar sensation, what is the peculiar quality of pleasure, which his work has the property of exciting in us, and which we cannot get elsewhere?'

Detail of *Venus and Mars* (plate 62)

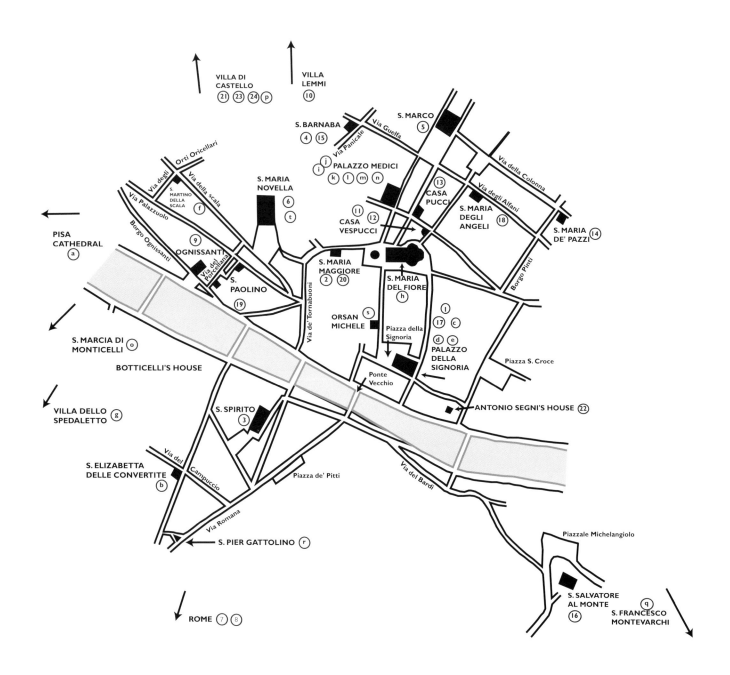

FLORENCE:

THE LOCATION OF BOTTICELLI'S WORKS IN THE 15TH CENTURY

Map

figure	Title of Picture	Plate number
1	Fortitude	6
2	St Sebastian	7
3	The Bardi Altarpiece	9
4	The San Barnaba Altarpiece	10
5	The Coronation of the Virgin	15
6	The Adoration of the Magi	22
7	The Adoration of the Magi	24
8	The Sistine Chapel frescoes	31-36, 38
9	St Augustine	39
10	The Villa Lemmi frescoes	41, 42
11	The Story of Virginia	43
12	The Story of Lucretia	44
13	The Story of Nastagio degli Onesti	51
14	The Annunciation	59
15	The Annunciation	60
16	The Raczinsky Tondo	52
17	Madonna of the Pomegranate	54
18	Madonna and Child with Three Angels	55
19	Pietà	61
20	The Panciatichi Pietà	63
21	Pallas and the Centaur	65
22	The 'Calumny' of Apelles	66
23	Primavera	67
24	The Birth of Venus	68

a	The Ascension of the Virgin (lost)	
b	The Convertite Altarpiece (lost or unidentified)	
c	The Adoration of the Magi (lost)	
d	Effigies of the Pazzi conspirators (lost)	
e	Audience Chamber frescoes (lost or never completed)	
f	The Annunciation (Uffizi, in store)	
g	Decorative frescoes (lost)	
h	Mosaic designs for vault of Chapel of St Zenobius (never completed, lost)	
i	Pallas (lost)	
j	Fortuna (lost)	
k	Bacchus (lost)	
l	Portrait of Simonetta Vespucci (lost)	
m	Portrait of Fioretta Gorini (lost)	
n	Portrait of Lucrezia Tornabuoni (lost)	
o	St Francis (lost)	
p	Decorative frescoes (lost)	
q	High altarpiece (lost or unidentified)	
r	High altarpiece (lost or unidentified)	
s	Baldacchino (lost)	
t	Design for embroidery (lost)	

CHRONOLOGY

Documented Events	Approximate Chronological Sequence of Pictures
1445 Birth of Alessandro Filipepi, later known as Botticelli, in Florence.	
1467 Filippo Lippi left Florence for Spoleto; Botticelli is believed to have been in his workshop before this date.	
1467–70	*Madonna and Child in a Mandorla of Seraphim* (Plate 1); *Madonna and Child in an Archway* (Plate 2); *Madonna and Child with Two Angels* (Plate 3); *The Adoration of the Magi* (Plate 17)
1470 The Pollaiuolo brothers and Botticelli painted *Virtues* for the hall of the Arte della Mercanzia.	*Forlitude* (Plate 6); *The Finding of the Dead Holofernes* (Plate 56); *The Return of Judith* (Plate 57); *Madonna and Child with an Angel with Symbols of the Eucharist* (Plate 4)
1472 Filippino Lippi was working as an assistant to Botticelli.	*Madonna and Child Enthroned with Six Saints* (Plate 8); *The Adoration of the Magi* (Plate 19)
1474 Botticelli went to Pisa (27 January).	*St Sebastian* (Plate 7); *The Adoration of the Magi* (Plate 22); *The Raczinsky Tondo* (Plate 52)
1478 The Pazzi conspiracy (26 April); Botticelli commissioned to portray the hanged criminals in fresco on the wall of the Palazzo Vecchio.	*Primavera* (Plate 67); *Abundance* (Plate 70); *St Augustine* (Plate 39); *The Annunciation* (Plate 58)

Documented Events	Approximate Chronological Sequence of Pictures
1481–82 Botticelli worked in Rome.	The Sistine Chapel frescoes (Plates 31-36, 38); *The Adoration of the Magi* (Plate 24); the Villa Lemmi frescoes (Plates 41 and 42); *The Birth of Venus* (Plate 68)
1483–84 Botticelli worked at the Medici Villa dello Spedaletto near Volterra on decorative frescoes.	*Portrait of a Young Man* (Plate 26); *Portrait of Giuliano de' Medici* (Plate 29); *Portrait of a Young Man Holding a Medallion* (Plate 28); *The Story of Nastagio degli Onesti* (Plate 51); *Pallas and the Centaur* (Plate 65)
1485	*The Bardi Altarpiece* (Plate 9); *Madonna of the Magnificat* (Plate 53); *Madonna and Child with a Book* (Plate 5)
1487	*Madonna of the Pomegranate* (Plate 54); *Portrait of a Man with a Medal* (Plate 27); *Portrait of Lorenzo Lorenzano* (Plate 30); *Venus and Mars* (Plate 62); *The San Barnaba Altarpiece* (Plate 10); *The Annunciation* (Plate 59)
1490	*The Coronation of the Virgin* (Plate 15); *Pietà* (Plate 61); *The Panciatichi Pietà* (Plate 63)
1491 Botticelli commissioned (18 May) to decorate vault of the Chapel of St Zenobius in Santa Maria del Fiore (his share of the work never completed); Botticelli acted as member of the committee to consider designs for façade of Santa Maria del Fiore.	*Three Angels* (Plate 69); *'Noli me Tangere'* (Plate 45); *The 'Calumny' of Apelles* (Plate 66); *'La Derelicta'* (Plate 40); *The Communion of St Jerome* (Plate 46); *St Augustine in his Cell* (Plate 37); *Madonna and Child with Three Angels* (Plate 55)
1496 Botticelli painted a fresco of St Francis in the dormitory of Santa Maria di Monticelli (the building destroyed 1529–30).	*Scenes from the Life of St Zenobius* (Plates 47–50) *Pentecost* (Plate 64)

Documented Events	Approximate Chronological Sequence of Pictures
1497 Botticelli and assistants commissioned to paint decorative frescoes for the Medici Villa di Castello.	
1497–1500	*The Annunciation* (Plate 60)
1500	*The Mystic Nativity* (Plate 21); *The Agony in the Garden* (Plate 25); *The Story of Virginia* (Plate 43); *The Story of Lucretia* (Plate 44); the *Divina Commedia* illustrations (Plates 71–74)
1504 Botticelli acted as member of the committee to decide on placing of Michelangelo's *David*.	
1510 Death of Botticelli; buried in Ognissanti (17 May).	

NOTE TO THE PLATES

All except one of Botticelli's paintings illustrated here are described as in tempera, that is, pigment suspended in an aqueous medium, usually egg. Where technical examinations of paintings have been made, notably in the case of the London *Adoration of the Magi* (Plate 17), it has been shown that the paintings also contain oil and oil and resin glazes carrying either dissolved dyestuffs, such as madder, or particles of pigment. The panel is probably poplar in most cases but only very rarely is the wood-type specified in museum catalogues.

Detail of *Madonna and Child with Two Angels* (Plate 3)

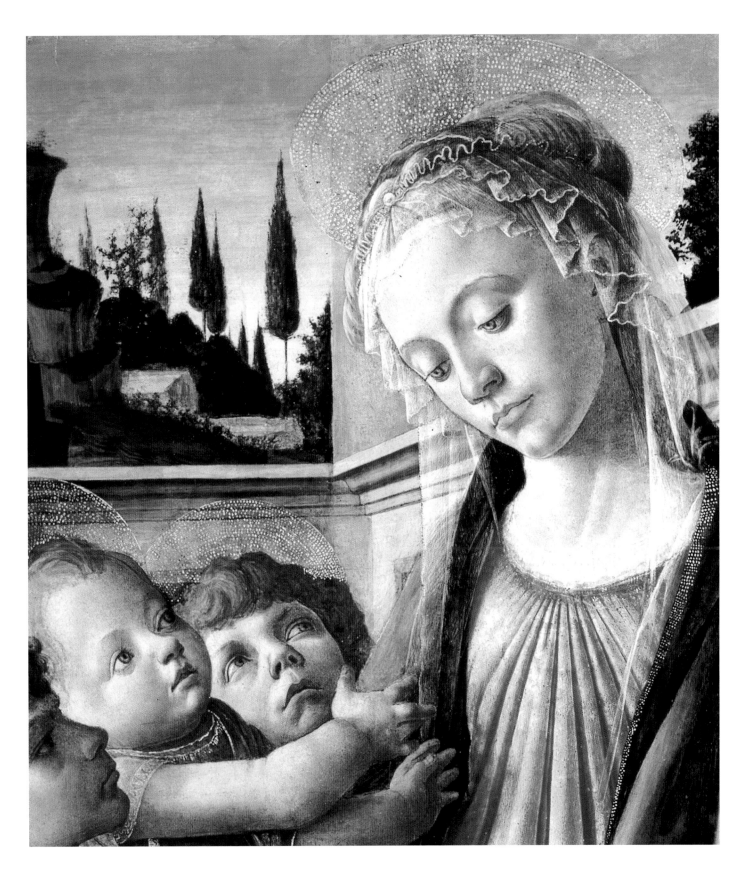

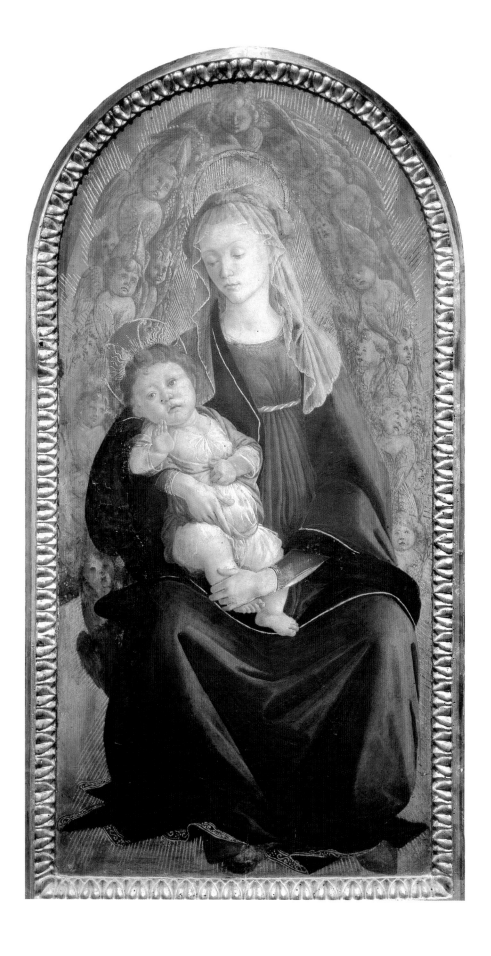

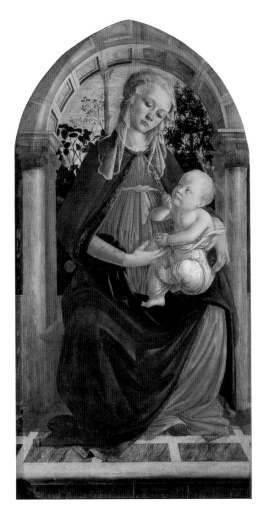

1 *Madonna and Child in a Mandorla of Seraphim*
FLORENCE, Galleria degli Uffizi.
Tempera on panel 120 x 65 cm.
Original frame. Suffering from rubbing, losses in areas of
gilding and a coating of discoloured varnish.

The early history of the panel is unknown, but it was
recorded without an attribution in a Uffizi inventory of
1784. In 1893 it was published in Ulmann's *Sandro Botticelli*,
since when it has been accepted as one of the artist's
earliest works, painted before the *Fortitude* (Plate 6) which
is known to have been finished by August 1470.
Diffidently composed, carefully excluding the complexities
of spatial description, this picture nevertheless
incorporates in embryonic form many of the stylistic
idiosyncrasies of Botticelli's mature work. The oversize
Child, for example, reappears only slightly refined in *The
San Barnaba Altarpiece* (Plate 10) of at least twelve years
later, and the uncomfortably long arm of the Madonna is
resolved as a graceful and positive feature of the design in
such figures as the Venus of *The Birth of Venus* (Plate 68).

(*above*)
2 *Madonna and Child in an Archway* (*Madonna del Roseto*)
FLORENCE, Galleria degli Uffizi.
Tempera on panel 124 x 64 cm.

This panel hung in the old Camera di Commercio on the
east side of the Piazza della Signoria before it was moved
to the Uffizi in the eighteenth century. Its original location
is unknown. It is a far more confident painting than the
Madonna and Child in a Mandorla of Seraphim (Plate 1), and
despite the fact that Morelli, in 1897, judged it a 'bastarda
opera', most authors agree in attributing it to Botticelli and
the period of the *Fortitude* (Plate 6), around 1470.

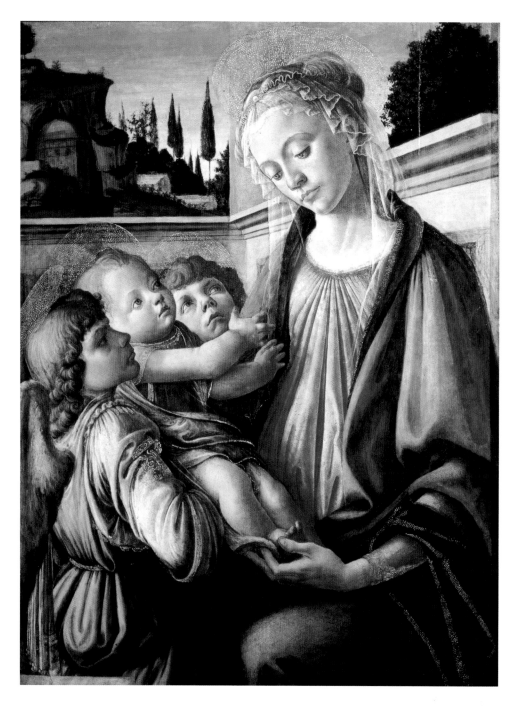

3 *Madonna and Child with Two Angels*
NAPLES, Gallerie Nazionale di Capodimonte.
Tempera on panel 100 x 71 cm.
Almost entirely repainted until restoration in 1957.

This *Madonna* was first recorded in 1697 in the Palazzo
Farnese, Rome, attributed to Filippino Lippi. The image
of two angels presenting Christ to his mother was derived
from Filippo Lippi and is best known in his *Madonna
Adoring the Divine Child* of 1457 in the Uffizi. Although
this picture by Botticelli still belongs to his earliest period
of 1468–70, a degree of finesse in the treatment of
draperies is already present. The Madonna's transparent
veil provides a foretaste of the dazzling brushwork which
later clothes the Graces in the *Primavera* (Plate 67).

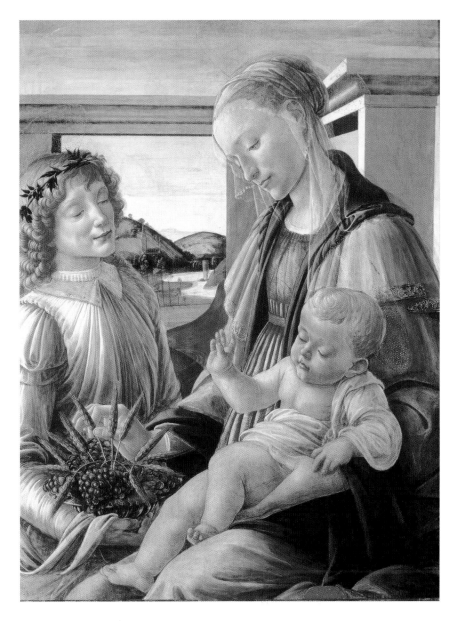

4 *Madonna and Child with an Angel with Symbols of the Eucharist (Madonna dell' Eucharista)*
BOSTON, Isabella Stewart Gardner Museum.
Tempera on panel 85 x 64.5 cm.

The composition of grapes and ears of wheat which the Child is blessing allude to the wine and bread of Communion. In the collection of the Principe Chigi, duca d'Ariccia, by the eighteenth century, this painting was sold in 1899 to Edmund Despretz. In the same year it was bought by Mrs Gardner through Berenson from Colnaghi in London. It arrived in Boston in 1901 after being exhibited in London. Sir Charles Eastlake recorded in his *Notebook I* of 1856 that he saw this *Madonna and Child*, a 'good composition', in the Palazzo Chigi, Rome, attributed to Ghirlandaio. Although he had difficulty judging its quality through the grime which then coated its surface, he considered it to be by Filippino Lippi or Botticelli. It is generally stated that Morelli confirmed in 1891 the 'traditional' attribution to Botticelli, but if Eastlake's notes are correct this tradition cannot have dated back earlier than 1856. It is quite possible that Eastlake was the first to propose the Botticelli attribution. The panel may date from the period immediately after the *Fortitude* (Plate 6) when Botticelli, as evidenced by the facial types, was still under the influence of Pollaiuolo and Verrocchio.

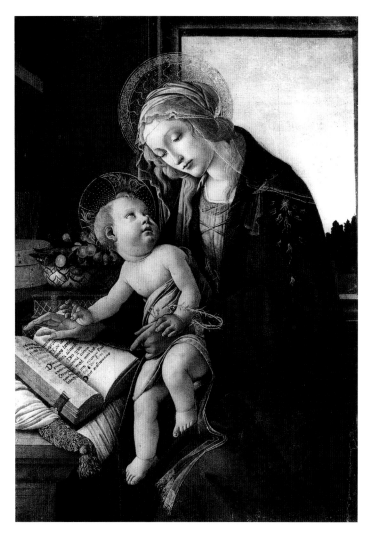

(above)
5 *Madonna and Child with a Book (Madonna del Libro)*
MILAN, Museo Poldi-Pezzoli.
Tempera on panel 58 x 39.5 cm.
Heavy overpainting removed in restoration of 1951.

For clarity of composition and tenderness of expression
this *Madonna* of the 1480s is unsurpassed
in Botticelli's *oeuvre*. It was first catalogued in the
Poldi-Pezzoli collection as a work of Botticelli in 1881,
and since then most scholars have recognized its
connection, both in terms of style and technique,
with the *Madonna of the Magnificat* (Plate 53).

6 *Fortitude*
FLORENCE, Galleria degli Uffizi.
Tempera on panel 167 x 87 cm.

Botticelli was paid in August 1470 for the *Fortitude* which
hung originally with six other *Virtues* by the Pollaiuolo
brothers in the hall of the Arte della Mercanzia in the
Piazza della Signoria, where magistrates sat for cases
arising from commercial transactions. Although it was
perhaps not immediately obvious to onlookers in the
magistrates' chamber that this graceful figure was
intended to epitomize strength and courage, they must
have admired the luxuriant architecture of the throne and
the glittering costume. Cavalcaselle, in 1894, was not,
however, impressed. He complained that the *Fortitude*
simply followed the other *Virtues* and shared 'Their
energy of movement, vulgarity of type and coarseness of
extremities and articulations'.

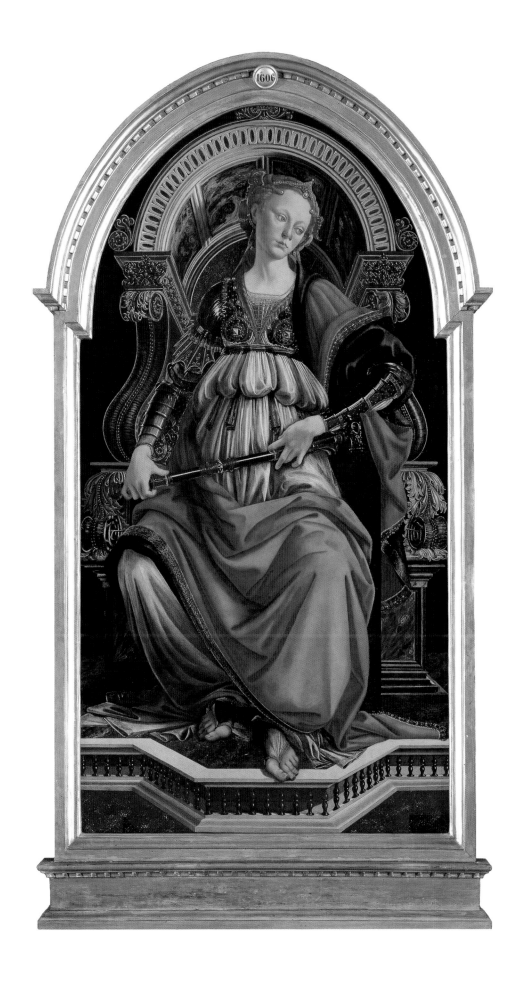

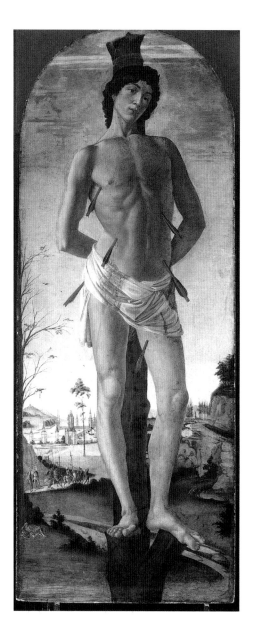

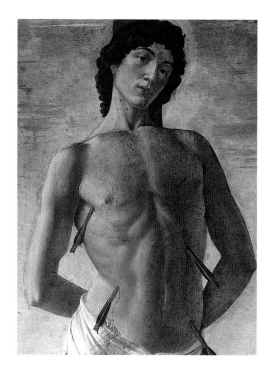

7 *St Sebastian*
BERLIN Gemäldegalerie.
Tempera on panel 195 x 75 cm.
Panel damaged at edges, particularly on the right.

According to the Anonimo Gaddiano this picture was hung on a pillar in the Church of Santa Maria Maggiore on 20 January 1474. It had gone from the church by the seventeenth century, and its history is unknown until it was acquired by the Berlin Museum with the Solly collection in 1821, attributed to Pollaiuolo. Unlike Mantegna, Tura, Antonello da Messina, Pollaiuolo and the majority of other fifteenth-century artists who painted St Sebastian, Botticelli did not seize on the legend that the saint was a member of the Roman Imperial Guard and accordingly embellish his scene with ostentatious classical paraphernalia. Instead, his backdrop to the figure is a sunny landscape with a strange little turreted harbour in the distance. There is a small but significant reference to militarism in the cavalcade of soldiers in the middle distance. One of the figures has just paused and shot an arrow right through a bird which plummets from the sky to its death. Botticelli perhaps intended this background incident to underline the central theme of the picture.

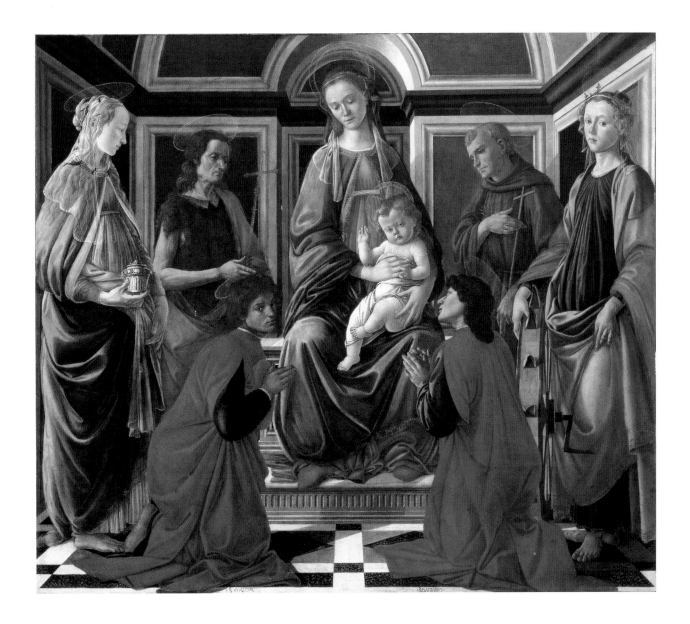

8 *Madonna and Child Enthroned with Six Saints*
FLORENCE, Galleria degli Uffizi.
Tempera on panel 170 x 194 cm.
Much sixteenth-century repainting, especially in areas of
Madonna and Child and two foreground saints.

After being moved from the Church of Sant' Ambrogio,
Piazza Sant' Ambrogio, to the Accademia, this picture
came to rest in the Uffizi in 1946. Early sources record a
panel by Botticelli in the Church of the Augustinian nuns
of Santa Elizabetta delle Convertite not far from the

Palazzo Pitti, a foundation for repentant prostitutes. A
number of scholars have associated this altarpiece with
the lost panel, but with the exception of Mary Magdalen
on the left, the other saints, John the Baptist, Francis,
Catherine and the Medici patrons Cosmas and Damian
have no obvious relevance to the mission of the nuns of
Santa Elizabetta. The faces of the two outermost female
saints are the only ones to have escaped overpainting, and
they suggest a date close to the *Madonna and Child with an
Angels with Symbols of the Eucharist* (Plate 4) in which the
Child is posed similarly.

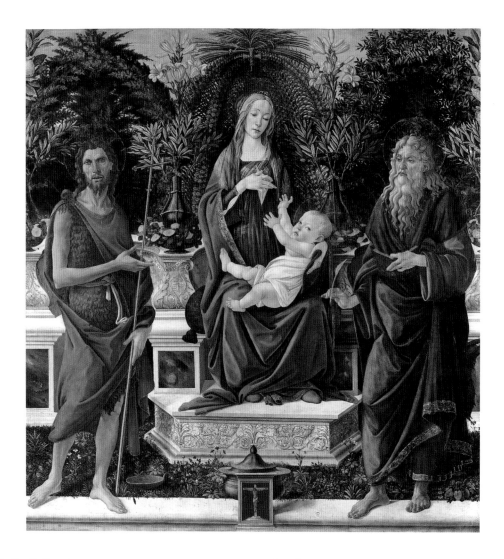

9 *The Bardi Altarpiece*
BERLIN Gemäldegalerie.
Tempera on panel 185 x 180 cm.

The Bardi Altarpiece is Botticelli's most immaculately
finished picture. It was commissioned by Giovanni
d'Agnolo de' Bardi in 1484–85 for his family chapel, the
first on the left on the end wall of the chancel of Santo
Spirito, now occupied by a gloomy *St Clare Communicates
before Christ* by the seventeenth-century painter Jacopo
Vignali. Botticelli received a final payment on 3 August
1485 of seventy-eight florins for the altarpiece. Earlier, on
7 February, Giuliano da Sangallo had received twenty-

four florins for carving the frame which is unfortunately
lost without trace. Sangallo later designed the sacristy of
Santo Spirito, which was begun in 1488. The picture
shows the two name saints of the donor, John the
Baptist, on the left, and John the Evangelist. The marble
bench-style throne in the picture recalls the seat on which
Filippo Lippi placed his *Seven Saints*, in the National
Gallery, London. Botticelli may have learnt from Lippi
not to have qualms about applying more than one eye
level to a composition. Here the four tall lily vases are
seen from below, yet the top ledge of the throne on
which they stand is seen from above.

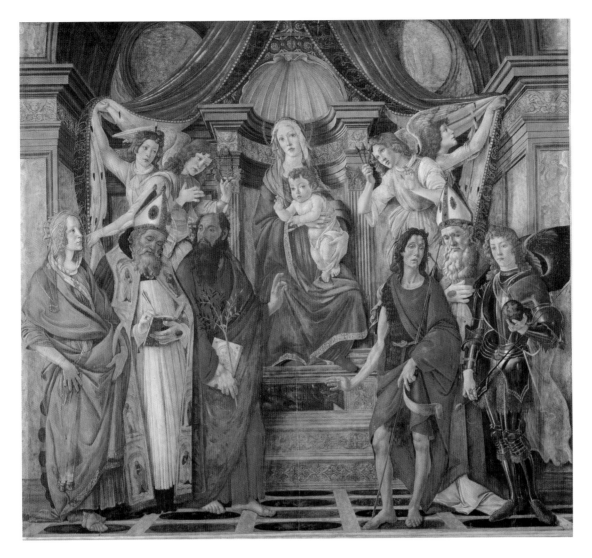

10 *The San Barnaba Altarpiece*
FLORENCE, Galleria degli Uffizi.
Tempera on panel 268 x 280 cm.
Cut at top edge; enlarged at top and base by Agostino
Veracini in 1717, additions removed after 1919; damage
to centre vertical join in panel affects faces of
Madonna and Child.

The full extent of Albertini's entry for San Barnaba in his
guide to Florence of 1510 reads 'In S. Barnaba there is a
large altarpiece by Sandro Botticelli, and other pictures.'
The painting was commissioned around 1488–90 by the
Guild of Medici e Speziali, patrons of the Church of San

Barnaba. It originally decorated the high altar, but by the
time of Cinelli's edition of Bocchi's *Belleze di Firenze*
(1677) it had been moved behind the altar. The date of
this move is sometimes erroneously given as 1700. When
the monastery and church were suppressed in 1808 the
altarpiece was placed in the Accademia and was
transferred from there to the Uffizi in 1919. As in *The
Bardi Altarpiece* (Plate 9) Botticelli chose a rich red as the
predominant hue and took pains to embellish the
composition with a magnificent variety of surfaces and
textures. The saints are, from the left, Catherine of
Alexandria, Augustine, Barnabas (with raised hand), John
the Baptist, Ignatius and Michael.

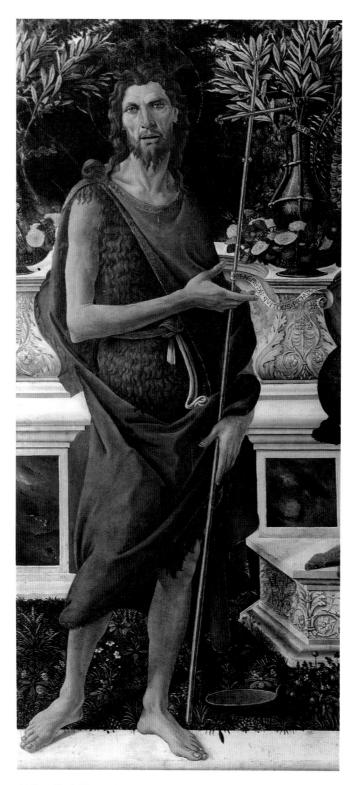

11 Detail of *The Bardi Altarpiece* (Plate 9)

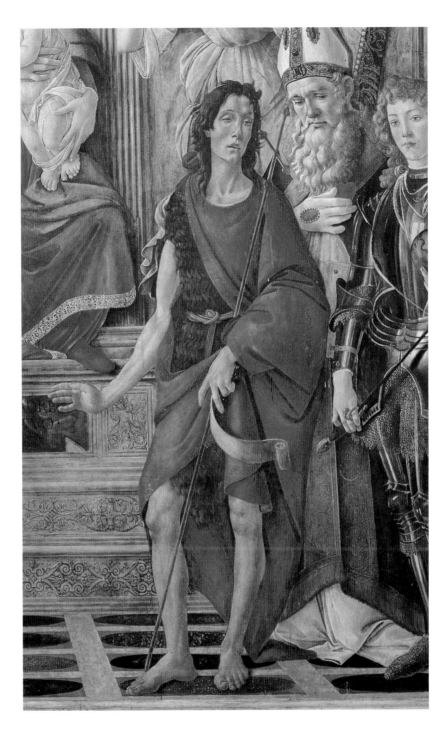

12 Detail of *The San Barnaba Altarpiece* (Plate 10).

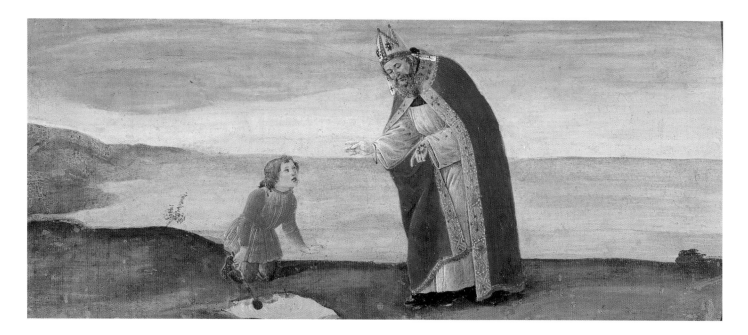

13 *The Vision of St Augustine*, predella panel of *The San Barnaba Altarpiece* (Plate 10) FLORENCE,
Galleria degli Uffizi.
Tempera on panel 20 x 38 cm.

Although the absence of any record of the original frame of *The San Barnaba Altarpiece* prevents an accurate reconstruction of the predella, the width of the picture and its composition suggests that there were seven separate panels. Of these four survive, all in the Uffizi. They depict *The Vision of St Augustine*, to correspond with the figure of St Augustine, second from the left in the

main panel, a *Pietà* for the centre piece, *Salome with the Head of the Baptist*, to be placed beneath St John, third from the right, and *The Removal of the Heart of St Ignatius*, positioned below the grey-bearded St Ignatius, second from the right. St Augustine, while meditating and trying to fathom the mystery of the Trinity, saw in a vision a child whose wish was to transfer the sea into one small hole. When Augustine told him this was impossible the child replied that it was no more futile than the saint's efforts to transfer the great mystery of the Trinity into his small brain.

14 *Sacred Scenes*, predella of *The Coronation of the Virgin* (Plate 15)
FLORENCE, Galleria degli Uffizi.
Tempera on panel 21 x 269 cm.

The original frame in which the predella was set does not survive. The scenes represented are *St John on the Island of*

Patmos, St Augustine in his Study, The Annunciation, St Jerome in the Desert and *St Eligius in his Workshop*, about to restore a foreleg to a horse and a nose to a lady. The last scene is related to a relief of the same subject by Nanni di Banco below his *St Eligius* on the exterior of Or San Michele.

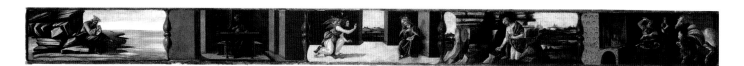

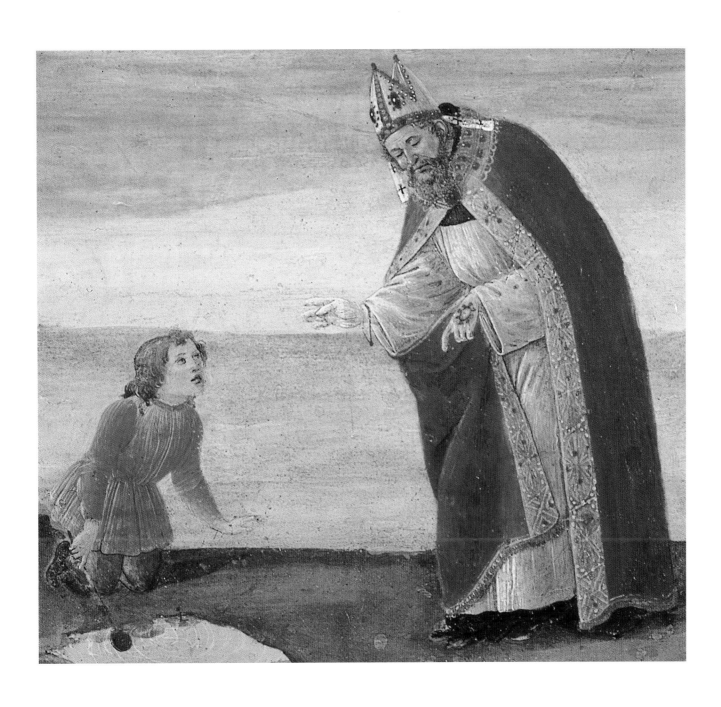

15 *The Coronation of the Virgin*
FLORENCE, Galleria degli Uffizi.
Tempera on panel 378 x 258 cm.

The Guild of Goldsmiths commissioned the picture between 1488 and 1490 for their Chapel of Sant' Alo on the left of the main door of the Church of San Marco. It was moved in 1596 to the Chapter of San Marco and then in 1807 to the Accademia. In 1919 it was transferred to the Uffizi. It is the only altarpiece by Botticelli to have retained its predella intact. As with *The San Barnaba Altarpiece* (Plates 10 and 12) the predella reflects incidents from the lives of the principal saints in the main composition, John the Evangelist, the Church Fathers Augustine and Jerome and the patron of goldsmiths, Eligius, familiar in Florentine art through the figure by Nanni di Banco on the west side of Or San Michele. *The Coronation of the Virgin* is the most grandiose and formal of Botticelli's altar panels. In critical history it has appealed to those who have found his art lacking in compositional structure. Cavalcaselle, for example, proclaimed almost with a sigh of relief that in this picture Botticelli 'succeeds in realizing at last the idea of infinity and space'.

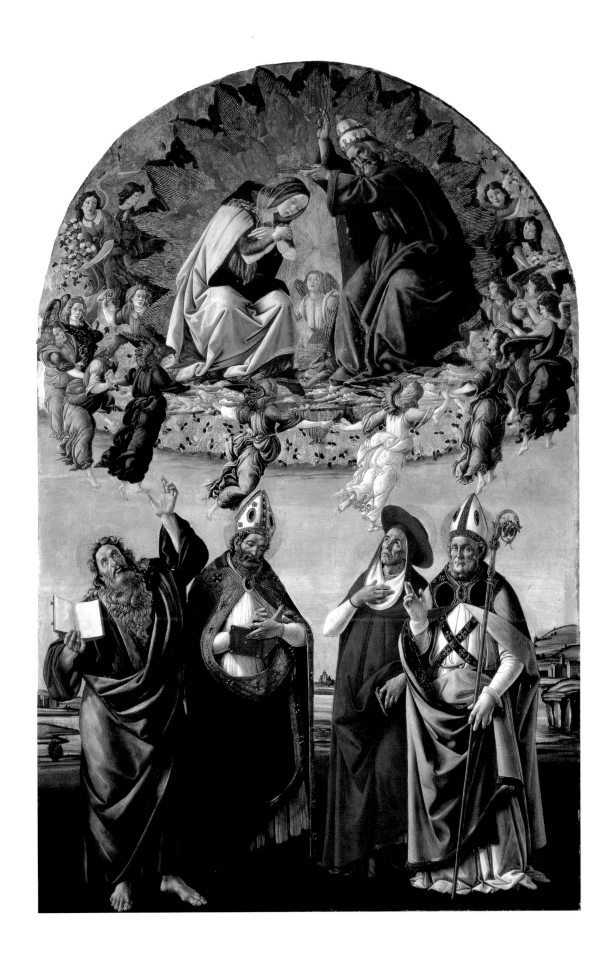

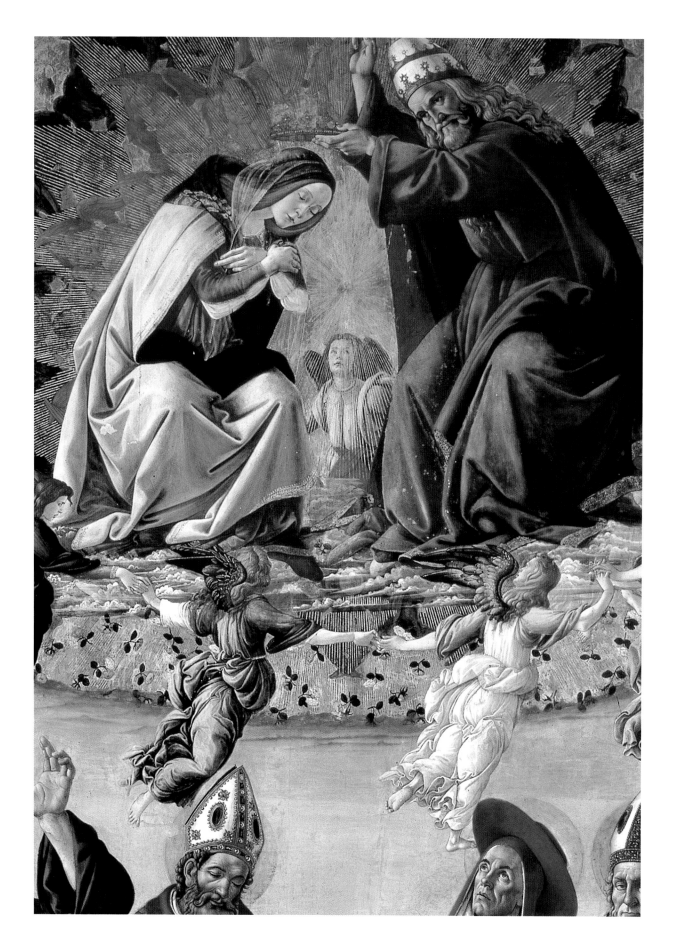

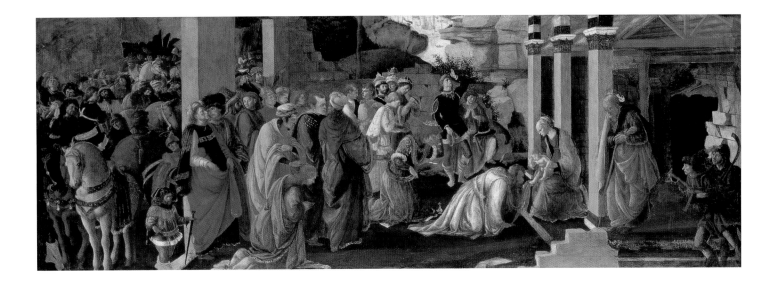

(*opposite*)
16 Detail of *The Coronation of The Virgin* (Plate 15)

In order to distinguish the heavenly from the earthly realms below, Botticelli brought back the seraphim of the earliest *Madonna* in the Uffizi (Plate 1) and added a semi-circle of dancing angels which looks forward to *The Mystic Nativity* (Plate 21). In a letter of 1876, the painter Edward Burne-Jones, yearning for another glimpse of this picture wrote, 'At the back of the Virgin the rays of gold rain on a most dear face that looks up and I want to see it . . .'

17 *The Adoration of the Magi*
LONDON, National Gallery.
Tempera on panel 50 x 136 cm. Two 2 cm. strips of paint added later at the left and right edges; restored 1940.

This is Botticelli's smallest and earliest *Adoration*. Its original home is unknown but it was in the Lombardi-Baldi collection, Florence, by 1845, and before that was in the possession of the Marchese Ippolito Orlandini of Florence. Eastlake purchased the picture with other items from the Lombardi-Baldi collection in 1857. It appears to date from before 1470. The numerous *pentimenti* and changes of technique have long puzzled scholars and even the detailed technical analysis made at the National Gallery after the picture was restored has far from settled the question of whether a second hand was responsible for some areas or whether Botticelli re-worked some of the figures himself at a later date. The scientific investigation did reveal that although the painting technique is in many respects experimental and varies from one group of figures to the next, it is at the same time highly skilful and inventive. The forms are built up in many successive layers of translucent pigment. The sleeve of the second kneeling king, for instance, is composed of no less than six layers of paint, some of which consist of pigment in a tempera medium and others of dyestuffs dissolved in an oil glaze. On the rough back of the panel are a drawing of a female figure holding a shield, part of a face and other scribbles, all possibly by Botticelli.

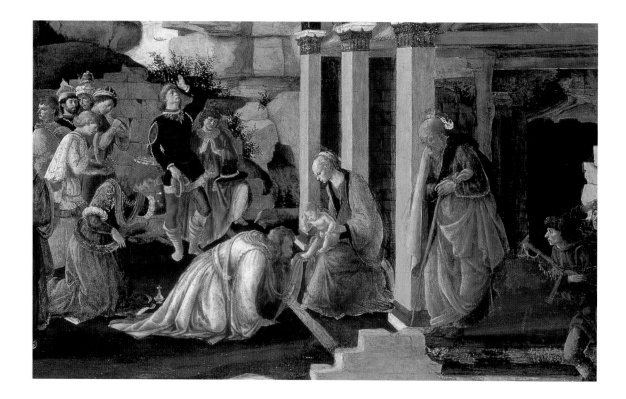

(above)
18 Detail of *The Adoration of the Magi* (Plate 17)

19 *The Adoration of the Magi*
London, National Gallery.
Tempera on panel (tondo) 131.5 cm. diameter. Slightly
rubbed; restored 1956.

The picture may be the one mentioned as being in the
Casa Pucci, Florence by Vasari in the 1568 edition of his
Vite. It was still in Florence, in the Palazzo Guicciardini in
1807. After passing through the Dubois and Coningham
collections it was recorded by Waagen as a work of
Filippo Lippi in the Fuller Maitland collection at Stansted
House, Essex in 1854. Morelli recognized the picture as
by Botticelli, but as Horne observed, the National Gallery
authorities 'thought fit to attribute it to Filippino Lippi'
after acquiring it in 1878 from Fuller Maitland for £800.
In the same year the National Gallery also bought *The
Mystic Nativity* (Plate 21) from him for £1500. Although
this *Adoration* is still an early picture it is one of Botticelli's
most ingeniously structured compositions. The Virgin, set
at the exact centre of the circle, is posed in the same way
as she is in *The San Barnaba Altarpiece* (Plate 10) of at least

fourteen years later. Also, as in the San Barnaba picture,
her importance is emphasized by the architectural
elements which surround and frame her, although in *The
Adoration* arched classical ruins take the place of the
interior church setting of the later *sacra conversazione*
composition. There is even in this *Adoration* an echo of
the inverted shell often found in formal interior groups as
part of the architecture above the Virgin's throne. A
similar semi-circular shape appears as a patch of sky seen
through the furthest arch above and behind the Madonna
and Child. The oversize peacock, which can also be seen
in the Lippi *Adoration* (fig. 10) in Washington and, rather
smaller, in Botticelli's Uffizi *Adoration* (Plate 22), was
probably intended to symbolize resurrection and
immortality, as the flesh of the peacock was supposed to
be immune to decay and this belief gave rise to the
association of the bird with immortal life in both pagan
and Christian iconography. The use of a resurrection
symbol in connection with the infant Christ is not
unusual; the pomegranate in the *Madonna of the
Pomegranate* (Plate 54) has the same connotation. As in the
early rectangular *Adoration* (Plate 17) a number of
pentimenti are visible in this tondo, especially in the sky
where the architecture once continued across to the
right edge.

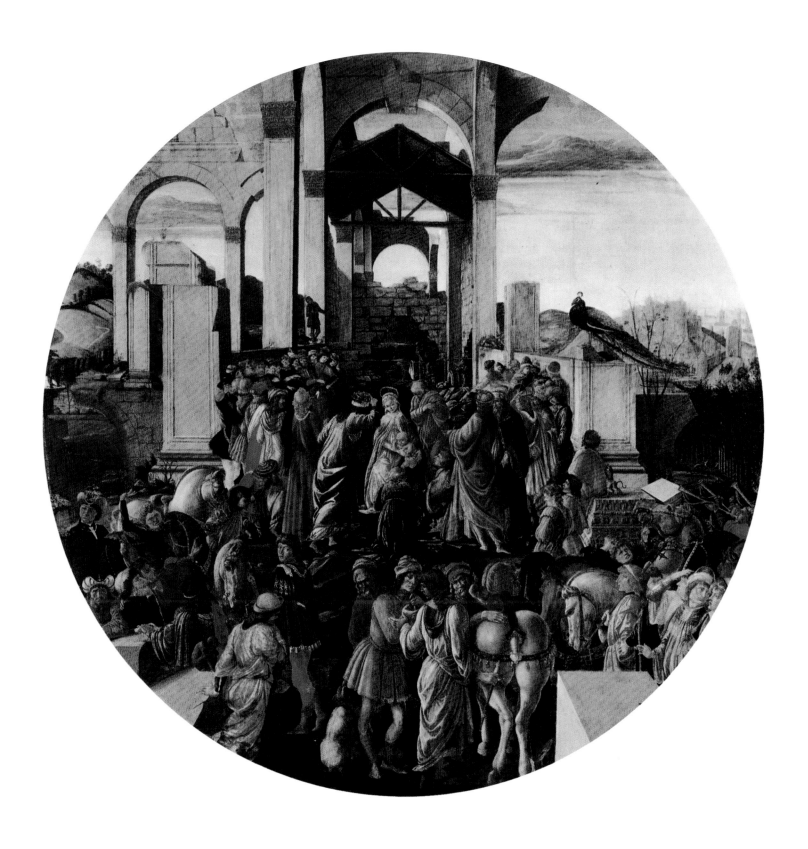

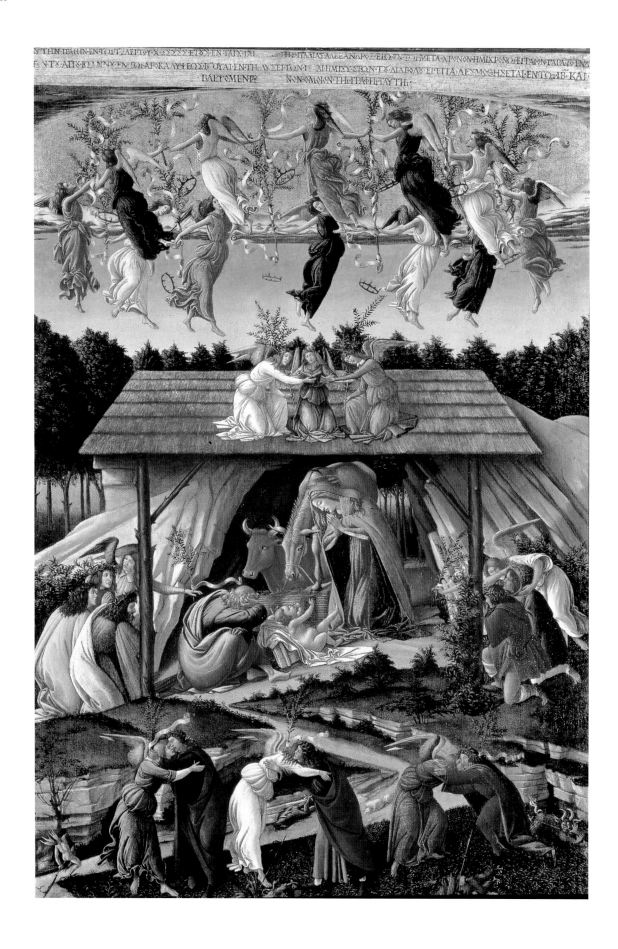

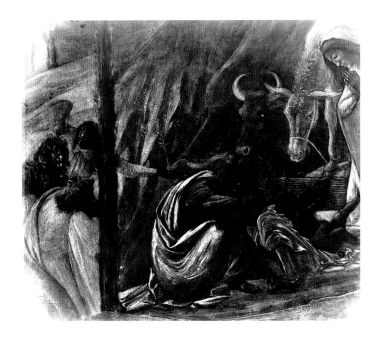

(above)
20 *The Mystic Nativity*
(X-ray photograph detail of left)
At the age of sixty-five and after over thirty years of experience Botticelli was still able to accept that the first marks he made with his brush were not always the right ones. In the course of painting the figure of St Joseph he completely changed the position of his right foot.

21 *The Mystic Nativity*
LONDON, National Gallery.
Oil (?) on canvas 108.5 x 75 cm.
Slightly damaged by flaking and wearing; restored 1958.

Like the tondo *Adoration* (Plate 19) *The Mystic Nativity* was purchased by the National Gallery from the Fuller Maitland collection, Stansted House, Essex in 1878. Fuller Maitland acquired it from Smith (1847) and before that it had been with Brown and in the Ottley collection, London. Ottley bought the picture from the Villa Aldobrandini in Rome, probably in the 1790s. It was the first picture by Botticelli to arrive in England correctly attributed, perhaps simply because it is the only one to be signed and dated. *The Times* of 2 October 1878, announcing the National Gallery's acquisition of *The Mystic, Nativity*, described the dancing angelic host as 'unquestionably the supreme expression of Botticelli's genius – one might almost say an invention unsurpassed in the whole range of art'. The signature is incorporated in the Greek inscription at the top of the picture: 'I Sandro painted this picture at the end of the year 1500 [?] in the troubles of Italy in the half time after the time according to the XIth chapter of St John in the second woe of the Apocalypse in the loosing of the devil for three and a half years then he will be chained in the XIIth chapter and we shall see clearly [?] . . . as in this picture'. The date is almost certainly intended to be the end of the year 1500. Much of the meaning of the inscriptions and images in this picture is obscure. The unusual feature of angels embracing three men holding and crowned with olive branches must be intended to illustrate Luke II: 14, 'Glory to God in the highest and peace, good will among men', a passage which is inscribed in Latin on the scrolls carried by the angels in the sky above. At the coming of Christ and the consequent good will among men, symbolized by the embracing figures, several devils are trying to hide themselves in fissures in the ground. It is not clear, however, in what way Botticelli meant them to relate to the apocalyptic passage referred to in the Greek inscription at the top of the picture. The reference is, in fact, not even accurate: the devil is not chained in the twelfth chapter of Revelation but in the twentieth. The 'troubles' have been variously interpreted as the disturbances in Florence following the death of Savonarola in 1498, the French invasion of northern Italy in 1499 or Cesare Borgia's invasion of the Romagna in the same year.

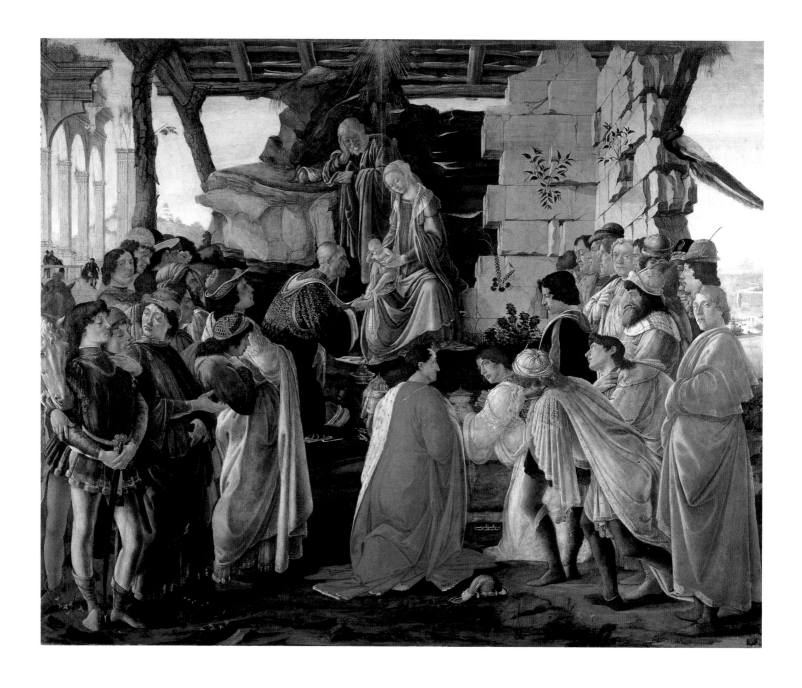

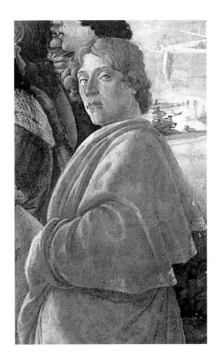

22 *The Adoration of the Magi*
FLORENCE, Galleria degli Uffizi.
Tempera on panel 111 x 134 cm. Scattered areas of discoloured retouching now visible.

The Uffizi picture is the only surviving *Adoration* for which early documentation exists. Vasari described how it hung above an altar between the two west doors of Santa Maria Novella, on the left as one entered the church by the centre door. It was commissioned around 1475–77 by Giovanni Lami of the Guild of Moneychangers, a close associate of the Medici. The patronage of the altar descended to the Fedini family and to a Spanish merchant, Mandragoni, who in turn sold the patronage of the altar to Bernardo Vecchietti who replaced Botticelli's *Adoration* with an *Annunciation* by Santi di Tito. *The Adoration* reappeared in the Medici Villa of Poggio Imperiale and was transferred to the Uffizi in 1796, attributed to Ghirlandaio. Vasari, who had a personal interest in the picture, having been employed by Mandragoni to refashion the altar surround, pointed out that the main figures of the kings and bystanders are portraits of the Medici. The king kneeling to kiss Christ's foot is Cosimo de' Medici and the other two kneeling kings his sons Piero, with the ermine gown, and Giovanni. Piero's sons Lorenzo 'il Magnifico' and Giuliano are believed to be the young man furthest left and the dark haired figure with downcast eyes, seen in profile to the front of the right hand group. A number of scholars have been tempted to identify the handsome man on the extreme right, looking out of the picture, as Botticelli himself.

(above)
Detail of *The Adoration of the Magi*

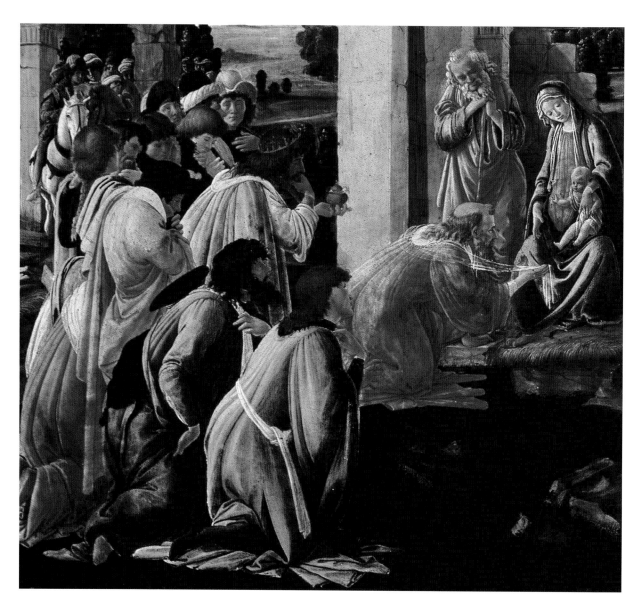

(*above*)
23 *Detail of The Adoration of the Magi* (Plate 24)

24 *The Adoration of the Magi*
WASHINGTON, National Gallery of Art
(Mellon collection).
Tempera on panel 70.2 x 104.2 cm.

A French engraver, Perallis, is thought to have acquired
the picture in Rome and from him it entered The

Hermitage, St Petersburg, in 1808 as a work of Mantegna.
It was recognized as a Botticelli by Waagen in 1864. After
being sold in 1933 it entered the Andrew W. Mellon
collection in 1937. It is usually believed to be the *Adoration*
which the Anonimo Gaddiano mentioned that Botticelli
painted while he was in Rome between 1481 and 1482
working in the Sistine Chapel (Plates 36 and 31–38).
Once again architecture is used to demonstrate the central
importance of the Madonna, but in this panel the actual
centre of the painted area is somewhat to the right of
the Virgin.

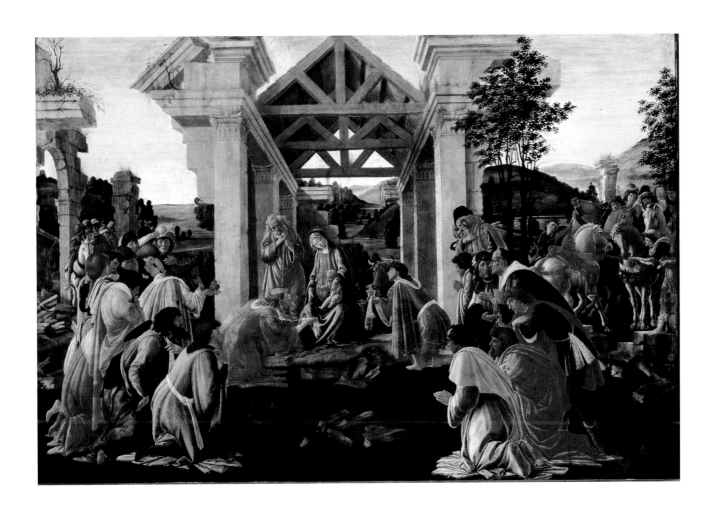

25 *The Agony in the Garden*
GRANADA, Capilla Real.
Tempera (?) on panel 53 x 35 cm.

Probably the first work by Botticelli to leave Italy *The Agony in the Garden* was listed among the works of art which Isabella I, 'the Catholic', Queen of Castile, commissioned, not long before her death in 1504, to decorate the Capilla Real in Granada. Stylistically the picture is very closely related to *The Mystic Nativity* (Plate 21), though it is only about half as large. The sleeping figure of St Peter on the left only has to turn his head to become the St Joseph of *The Mystic Nativity*, and the olive branches carried by angels in *The Mystic Nativity* could well have been plucked from the trees which surround Christ in the Garden of Gethsemane. This poignant and beautiful picture has received scant attention in the literature presumably because it happens to be in Spain, rather than because it is in any way unworthy of the artist.

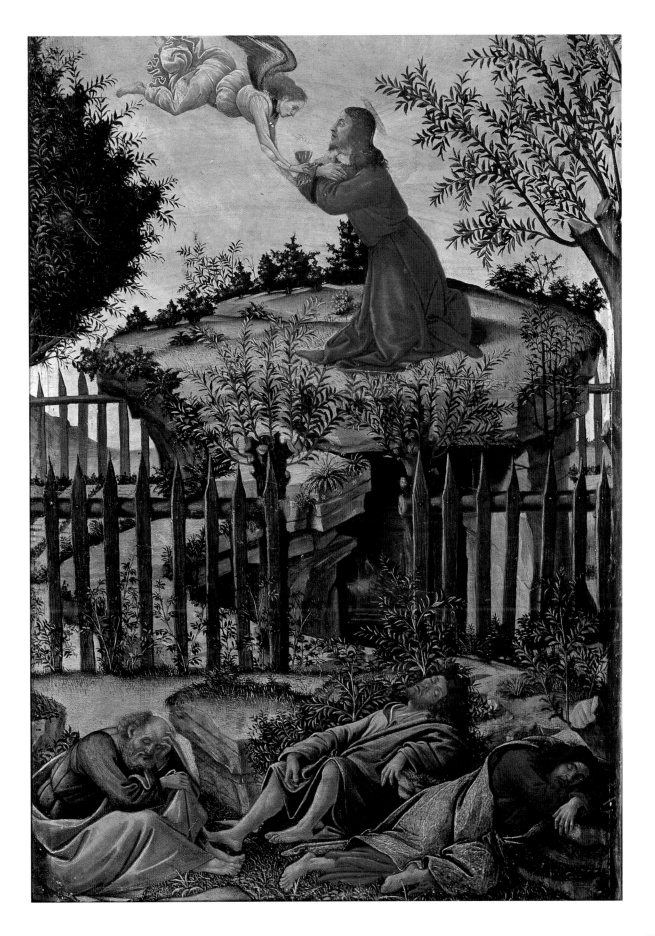

26 *Portrait of a Young Man*
LONDON, National Gallery.
Tempera on panel 37.5 x 28.2 cm. Cleaned 1968.

Sold as a self portrait by Masaccio at the Colonel
Matthew Smith sale, 12 May 1804, to Lord Northwick,
the picture was subsequently purchased from the
Northwick sale by the National Gallery in 1859 and
attributed to Botticelli in 1881. Julia Cartwright, in 1903,
admired the young man for 'his bright and pleasant
countenance and keen intellectual air'. The painting used
to be disfigured by black spots on the flesh. It is likely
that these were small bubbles which formed and burst
during the painting and filled with dirt over the centuries.
During treatment it was found that the picture is, unlike
some others such as the early *Adoration of the Magi* (Plate
19), very simple in technique. The flesh, for example, is of
one paint layer only. The picture probably dates from the
early 1480s.

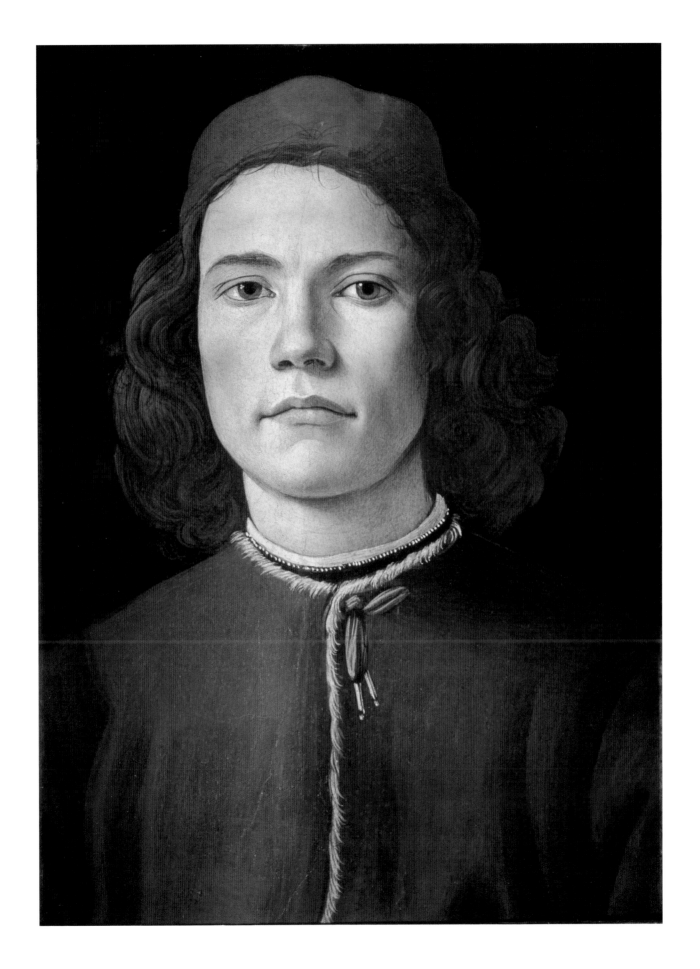

27 *Portrait of a Man with a Medal*
FLORENCE, Galleria degli Uffizi.
Tempera on panel 57.5 x 44 cm.

The man holds a posthumous medal of Cosimo de' Medici, which is actually a cast set into the panel and gilded. Suggestions for the identification of the sitter, ranging from Pico della Mirandola to Botticelli's brother, are as varied as proposals for dating, from before 1470 to 1492. The man is very similarly dressed to that in the *Portrait of a Young Man* (Plate 26), but in almost every other respect the two pictures are quite unalike. The *Man with a Medal* has an air of vitality derived both from the pose of the figure, with the head turned slightly away from full face, and from the outdoor setting, which makes the London *Young Man* appear rather stiff and two-dimensional by contrast.

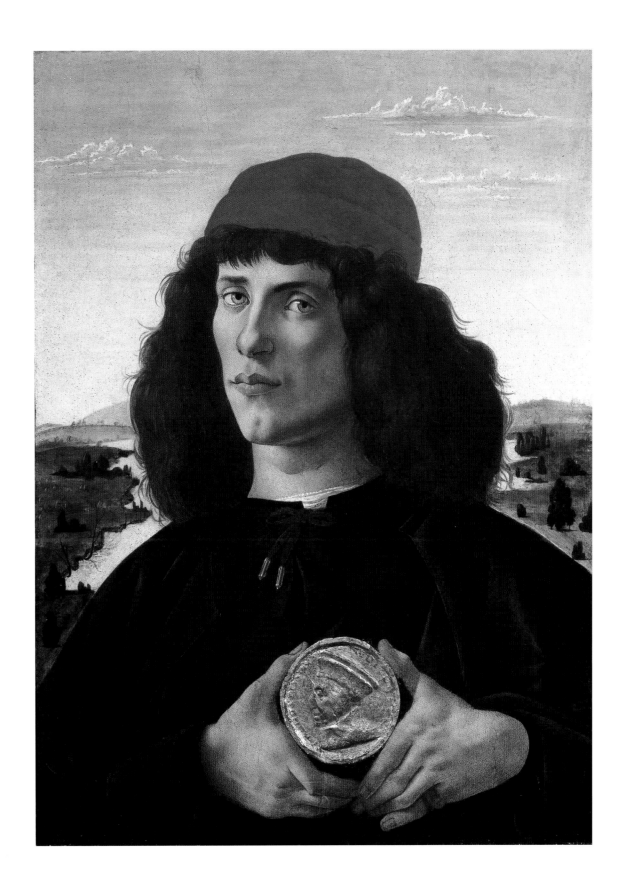

28 *Portrait of a Young Man Holding a Medallion*
Lent to the National Gallery, Washington.
Tempera on panel 58.4 x 39.4 cm.

Before entering the collection of Sir Thomas Merton, the picture belonged to Lord Newborough of Glynlivon Park, Caernarvon. It had been in the hands of his family since the time of the first Lord Newborough (1736–1807), who had lived for a time in Tuscany. The young man was identified by Scharf in a privately printed catalogue of the Merton collection (1950) as Giovanni di Pierfrancesco de' Medici (1467–1498), brother of Lorenzo di Pierfrancesco, but there is no real evidence to support this identification. The circular medallion fragment of an earlier picture, which is physically set into Botticelli's panel, has been attributed to the Ovile Master, dateable around 1350, in a note in the catalogue to an exhibition, Italian Art in Britain, at the Royal Academy, London, in 1960. The picture has not yet undergone technical tests, but when it does it may be possible to ascertain whether the inset fragment was put in the picture by Botticelli or whether the young man originally held a cast of a medal like the one in the Uffizi portrait (Plate 27).

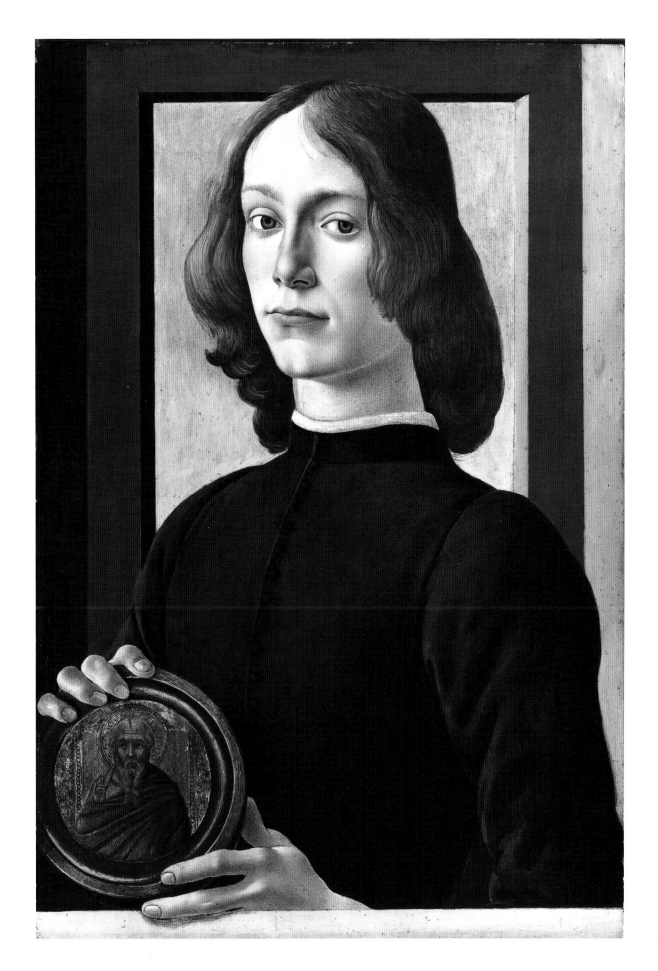

29 Portrait of Giuliano de' Medici
WASHINGTON, National Gallery of Art
(Samuel H. Kress collection).
Tempera on panel 75.6 x 52.6 cm. Cleaned 1950.

Formerly in the collection of Conte Vittorio Cini, Venice, this portrait passed through Wildenstein, New York, to Samuel Kress in 1949. Versions of the picture exist in the Gemäldegalerie, Berlin, and in the Accademia Carrara, Bergamo and another, with the figure facing the left, is in the Crespi collection, Milan. Only the Washington picture has the dove on a dead branch in the foreground and the shuttered window, both symbols of death. Giuliano, the younger brother of Lorenzo 'il Magnifico', was murdered in Florence in 1478 at the age of twenty-five in the Pazzi conspiracy, possibly organized with the connivance of the della Rovere pope, Sixtus IV. He is shown in this picture in profile with downcast eyes as in *The Adoration of the Magi* (Plate 24) and it is possible that all four versions of the portrait are posthumous studies based on sources such as drawings for *The Adoration*. The Washington picture appears to be the most accomplished of the versions.

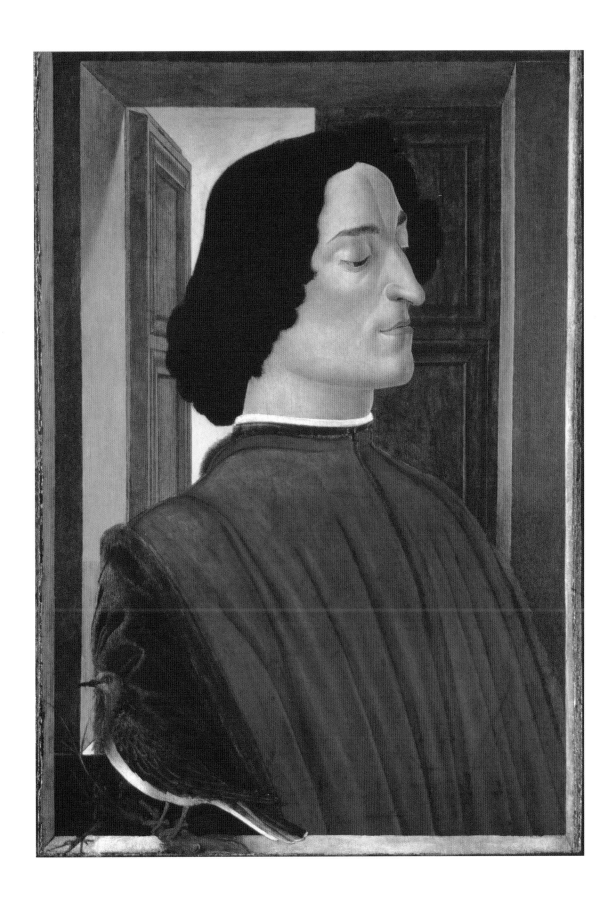

30 *Portrait of Lorenzo Lorenzano*
PHILADELPHIA, Philadelphia Museum of Art
(John G. Johnson collection).
Tempera on panel 50.8 x 36.5 cm.
Over-cleaned and extensively retouched.

The picture was purchased in 1909 by Johnson from
Baron Lazzaroni, Paris, on the recommendation of
Berenson. It is inscribed at the top: L. LORENTIANO.
Lorenzano was a highly regarded scholar associated with
the Medici circle. He held the chair of dialectics and then
of physics and medicine at the University of Pisa. He
committed suicide by throwing himself down a well in
1502. His date of birth is unknown. The picture is usually
dated between 1485 and 1490.

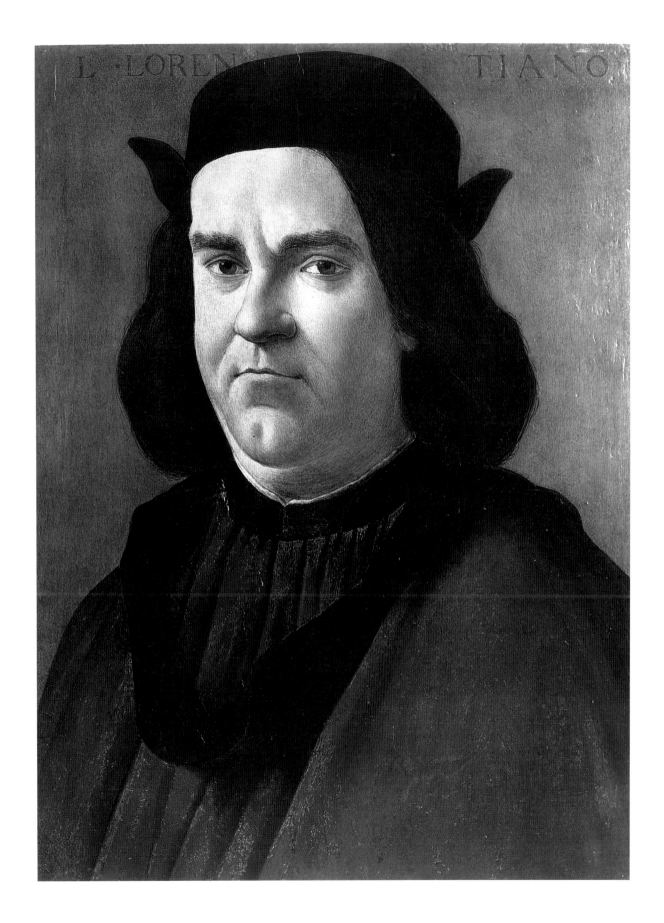

31 *General View of the Sistine Chapel*
VATICAN CITY.

The Sistine Chapel was built in Rome between 1475 and
1481, during the pontificate of Sixtus IV della Rovere,
under the direction of the clerk of the works Giovanni
dei Dolci, with Baccio Pontelli as architect. It is
approximately forty metres long, thirteen metres wide and
twenty-six metres high. Dolci was also responsible for
overseeing the decoration, and it was he who in 1481
made arrangements with Botticelli, Ghirlandaio, Cosimo
Roselli and Perugino to decorate the four walls with a
frieze of scenes from the life of Moses and from the life
of Christ and, between the windows, figures of martyred
popes. There were originally sixteen principal scenes (see
diagram). Four were finished by 17 January 1482 and a
further ten by October 1482. The last two were executed
by Signorelli who was probably brought in towards the
end of 1482, after the other artists had left for Florence
where on 5 October they were commissioned to paint the
Sala dei Gigli of the Palazzo Vecchio. The ceiling of the
Sistine Chapel was originally to have been a starry sky
executed by the Umbrian painter Piermatteo d'Amelia,
but there is no concrete evidence that it was ever
executed. *The Life of Moses* scenes occupy the left side of
the chapel. They began on the altar wall, now covered by
Michelangelo's *Last Judgement*, with a *Finding of Moses* by
Perugino, and ended on the opposite wall with a *Dispute
over the Body of Moses* by Signorelli, later repainted by
Matteo da Lecce. *The Life of Christ* scenes, arranged in
typological sequence opposite *The Life of Moses*, began on
the right of the altar wall with a *Nativity* by Perugino and
ended with a *Resurrection* by Ghirlandaio, also repainted by
Matteo da Lecce. The altarpiece was an *Assumption* by
Perugino. Michelangelo's decorative scheme was
commissioned during the pontificate (1503–13) of the
second della Rovere pope, Julius II, and all that remains
today of the original decoration from the time of Sixtus
IV are the twelve scenes from *The Life of Moses* and *The
Life of Christ* and the series of *Popes* on the lateral walls.

	Perugino The Finding of Moses	**Perugino** The Nativity (lost)	
Perugino and Pinturicchio The Journey of Moses into Egypt	**ALTAR** **Perugino** The Assumption (lost)		**Perugino** The Baptism of Christ
Botticelli Moses in the Desert: his Vocation (Plate 33)			**Botticelli** The Temptation and the Purification of the Leper (plate 34)
Cosimo Roselli The Passage of the Red Sea			**Ghirlandaio** The Vocation of Peter and Andrew
Cosimo Roselli (workshop) Moses and the Tables of the Law			**Cosimo Roselli and Piero di Cosimo** The Sermon on the Mount
Botticelli The Punishment of the Rebels (Plate 36)			**Perugino** The Presentation of the Keys to Peter
Signorelli The Death of Moses			**Cosimo Roselli** The Last Supper
	Signorelli The Dispute over the Body of Moses	**Ghirlandaio** The Resurrection (lost)	

*Diagram of the Original Scheme of the Sistine Chapel
(not to scale)*

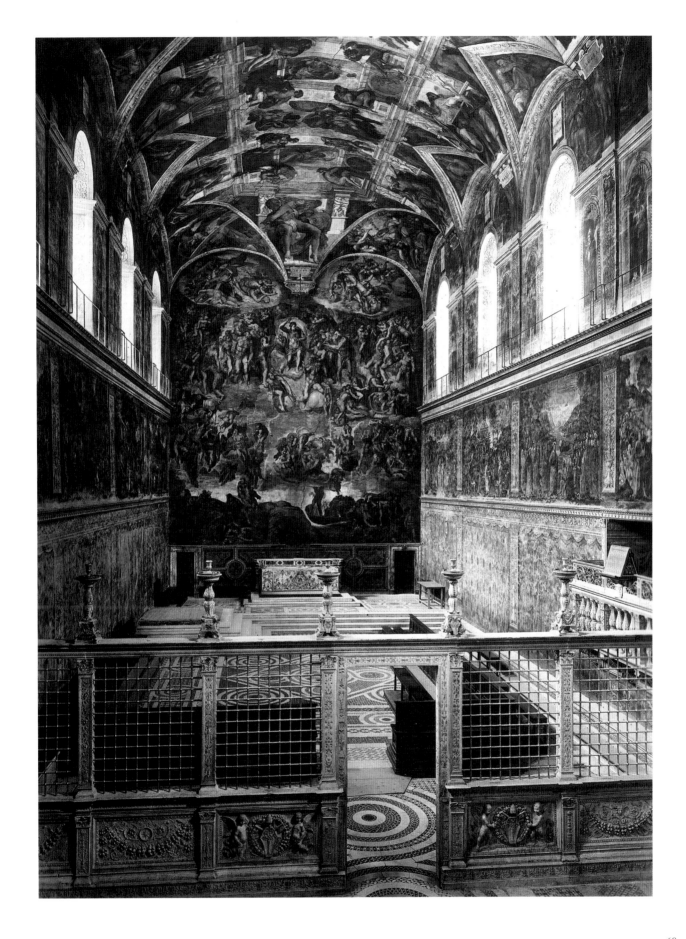

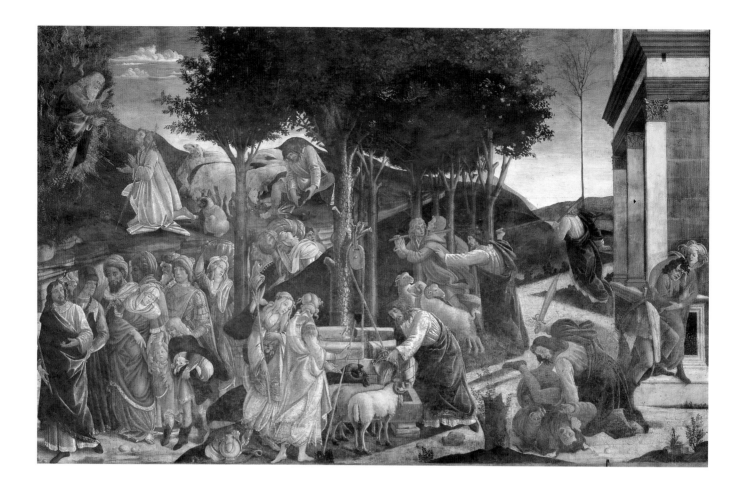

32 *Moses in the Desert: his Vocation*
VATICAN CITY, Sistine Chapel.
Fresco 348.5 x 558 cm.

The Life of Moses series of frescoes reads from the altar from right to left. Botticelli's first contribution to the left wall is *Moses in the Desert*, the second fresco between *The Journey of Moses into Egypt* by Perugino and Pinturicchio and *The Passage of the Red Sea* by Cosimo Roselli (see diagram, p. 68). Botticelli depicted Moses seven times, first on the right, killing an Egyptian (Exodus II, 11 ff.) and then fleeing from Pharoah to the land of Midian where, by a well (centre) he drove away shepherds who

had prevented the daughters of Jethro from watering their flock (Exodus II, 15 ff.). Jethro subsequently took Moses into his family, and it was while Moses was guarding Jethro's flock that God called to him from a burning bush (Exodus III, I ff.) and commanded him 'put off your shoes from your feet, for the place on which you are standing is holy ground'. The last episode represented by Botticelli is on the left, the return of Moses with his family to Egypt (Exodus IV, 19 ff.).

(opposite)
33 Detail of *Moses in the Desert: his Vocation.*

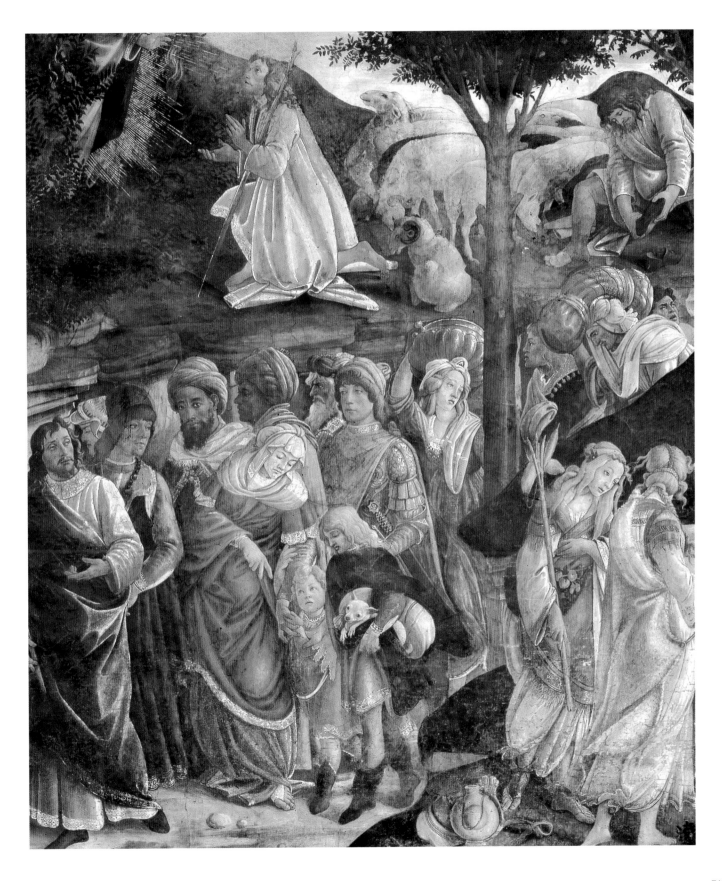

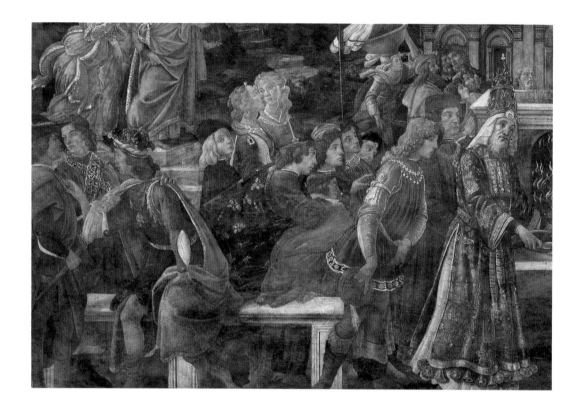

34 *The Temptation and the Purification of the Leper*
VATICAN CITY, Sistine Chapel.
Fresco 345.5 x 555 cm.

Although in theological terms the Moses story precedes
and foreshadows the life of Christ, in the Sistine Chapel,
The Life of Christ on the right wall was painted first.
Botticelli's *Temptation* is the second fresco from the altar
on the lateral wall directly opposite his *Moses in the Desert*
(Plate 32) (see diagram, p. 68). The temptations are
depicted in the background. First, the devil, on the left,
subtly disguised in a monk's habit, attempts to persuade
Christ to turn stones into bread (Matthew IV, 1–4). He
then (Matthew IV, 5–7) tries to cajole Christ into leaping
from the pinnacle of the Temple of Jerusalem,

represented in the fresco as the Hospital of Santo Spirito,
built by Sixtus IV. Finally (top right), the devil is driven
away after offering in vain all the kingdoms of the earth
(Matthew IV, 8–11). The main scene in the foreground
shows the leper cured by Christ making an offering of
thanksgiving (Matthew VIII, 1–4). Agostino Taja in his
description of the Vatican of 1750 noted especially how
the figures in this fresco are all in 'belle attitudini'. Many
attempts have been made to identify figures in the
composition with contemporaries and relations of Pope
Sixtus IV.

(above)
35 Detail of *The Temptation and the Purification of the Leper*.

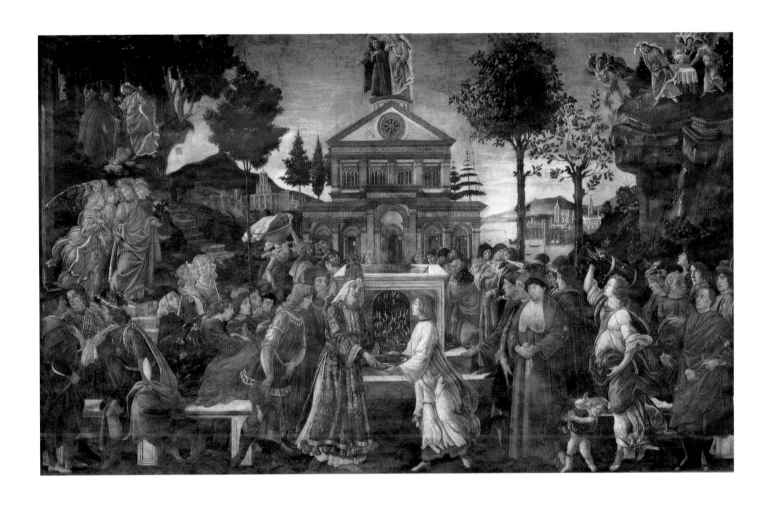

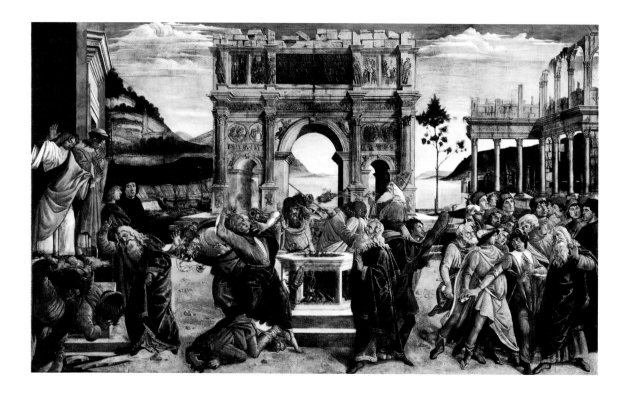

(*above*)
36 *The Punishment of the Rebels*
VATICAN CITY, Sistine Chapel.
Fresco 348.5 x 570 cm.

The Punishment of the Rebels is the fifth fresco on the left wall of the Sistine Chapel (see diagram, p. 68) and the most dramatic of the three by Botticelli. Korah and his sympathizers, who refuse to accept the authority of Aaron, are summoned by Moses to appear carrying censers before Aaron. On the right of the picture the followers of Moses and Aaron retreat as 'the earth opened up its mouth' and swallowed 'all the men that belonged to Korah and all their goods'. According to the Biblical source (Numbers XVI, 1–40) the confrontation took place at the entrance of a tent, but Botticelli placed it before the Arch of Constantine on which are emblazoned the words 'Nobody takes honour on himself unless like Aaron called by God' ('NEMO SIBI ASSUMM / AT HONOREM NISI VOCATUS A DEO / TANQUAM ARON').

37 *St Augustine in his Cell*
FLORENCE, Galleria degli Uffizi.
Tempera on panel 41 x 27 cm.

In this picture a bright curtain is drawn back to give us a glimpse of a small ageing neighbourly figure only distantly related to the ecstatic *St Augustine* of Ognissanti (Plate 39). It may be that the curtained-off sculptural setting was inspired by triumphal-arch style wall-tombs created earlier in the century by the Rosellino brothers, such as the Cardinal of Portugal's monument in San Miniato al Monte. The picture is believed to be the one mentioned by Vasari as by Filippo Lippi in the house of Bernardo Vecchietti. In the eighteenth century Ignazio Hugford of Florence sold it to Piero Pieralli, from whom it passed to the Uffizi in 1779.

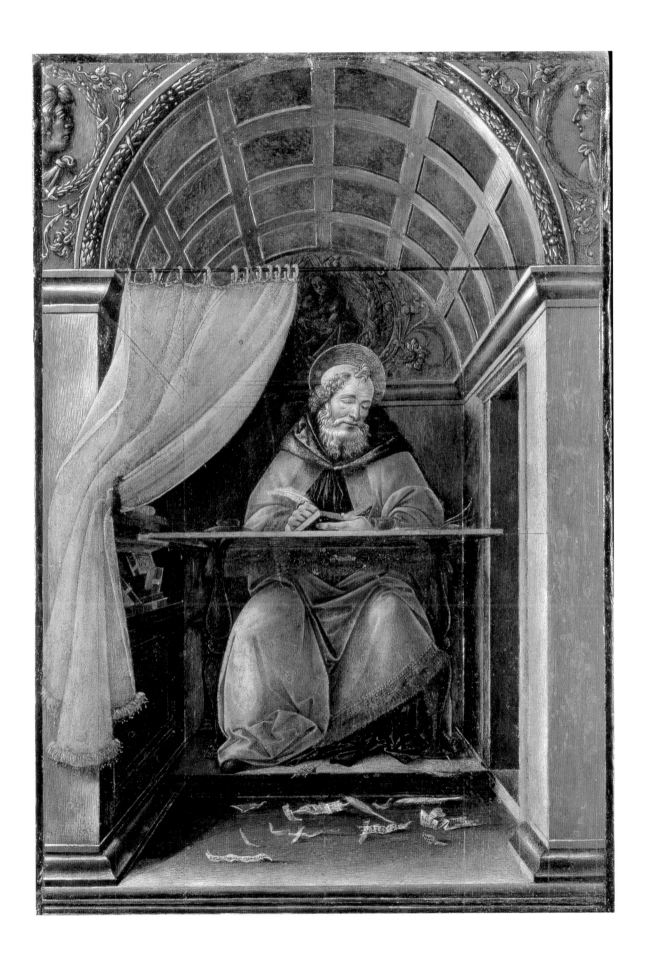

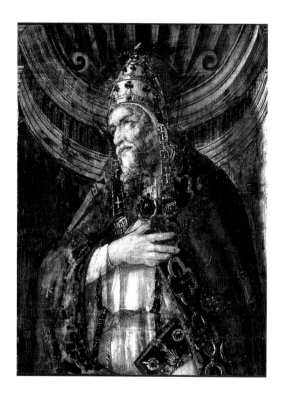

(above)
38 *Detail of St Sixtus II*
VATICAN CITY, Sistine Chapel. Fresco 210 x 80 cm. (total measurement). Damaged and retouched.

Botticelli and his assistants had a hand in eleven of the twenty-eight existing *Popes* placed in painted niches at window level above the main frieze of scenes from *The Life of Moses* and *The Life of Christ*. Many of the *Popes* are badly damaged, and the *St Sixtus* is repainted from the waist down and in details such as the hand, held to the breast in much the same attitude as that of the *St Augustine* (Plate 39) of Ognissanti.

39 *St Augustine*
FLORENCE, refectory of the Monastery of Ognissanti. Fresco 152 x 112 cm.

Painted in 1480 for a member of the Vespucci family, perhaps Giorgio Antonio Vespucci, canon of the Cathedral of Florence, this fresco originally decorated the screen of the monks' choir in the Church of Ognissanti.

When the screen and other mediaeval embellishments were removed under the direction of the Grand Duke Cosimo I de' Medici of Tuscany between 1564 and 1566 the *St Augustine* and its pendant *St Jerome* by Ghirlandaio were moved to the walls of the nave. The *St Augustine* was set between the third and fourth altars on the right wall. After the 1564 detachment the inscription on the frieze was added: 'Augustine has devoted himself so completely to sacred studies that he is not aware that his location has been changed.' Since then he has moved again. Ognissanti was one of the many churches inundated by the disastrous flood of 1966 and although the *St Augustine* and *St Jerome* were not very seriously damaged, they were removed from the church, restored and repositioned on the right and left walls of the refectory, on either side of Ghirlandaio's famous *Last Supper*. The losses to the lower part of the draperies of *St Augustine* are not flood damage; they are clearly visible in earlier photographs. Several scholars have proposed that both Botticelli's and Ghirlandaio's compositions may have been influenced by a small *St Jerome in his Study* by Jan van Eyck known to have been in the Medici collection in the fifteenth century but now lost.

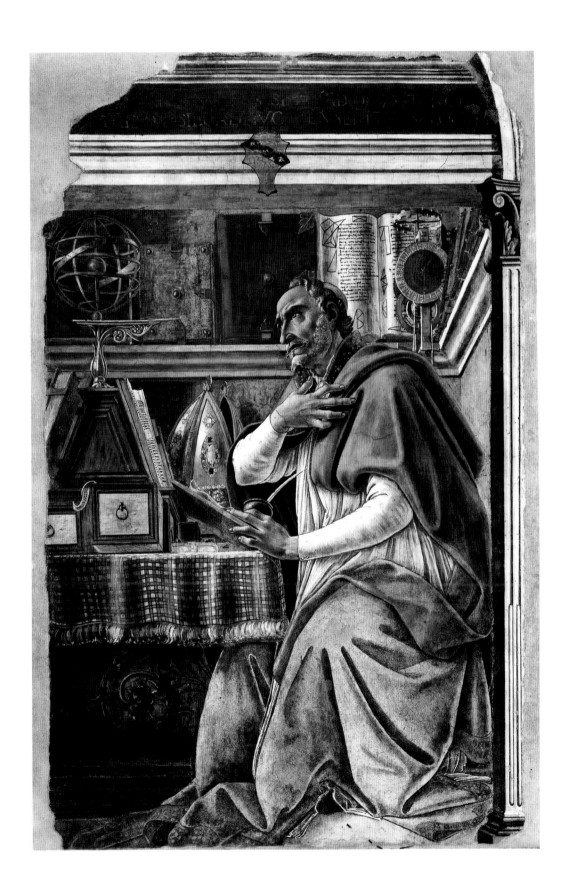

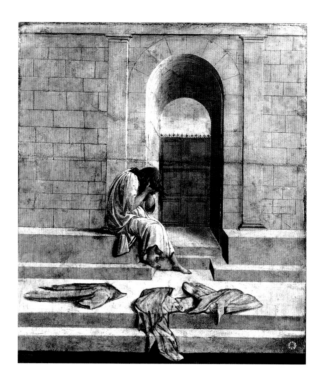

40 *'La Derelicta' (above)*
ROME, Galleria Pallavicini-Rospigliosi.
Tempera on panel 47.3 x 42.8 cm.

Although Federico Zeri's catalogue of the Galleria Pallavicini of 1959 attributes the picture to Filippino Lippi, most writers consider this mysterious little panel to be by Botticelli. It was acquired by the Principe Giuseppe Rospigliosi in 1816 as a work of Masaccio and since that date numerous proposals for the identification of the subject have been made, none of which can be verified until some clue from the early history of the picture is found.

41 *Young Man before the Liberal Arts*
PARIS, Musée du Louvre.
Fresco (detached) 227 x 269 cm.
Extensively damaged.

In 1873 three frescoes were discovered under whitewash in the Villa Lemmi, a house in Chiasso Macerelli, a road on the outskirts of Florence leading from near Ponte a Rifredi to San Pietro a Careggi. One fresco, a ruin, remains in the villa, but the other two were moved to the Louvre in 1882 suffering damage in the process. The frescoes used to be associated with the marriage of Giovanna degli Albizi and Lorenzo Tornabuoni in 1486 but several scholars, and principally Gombrich, in 1945, have cast doubt on this connection, pointing out that the young woman in the second fresco (Plate 42) does not resemble authentic representations of Giovanna, and that there is no certainty that the Villa Lemmi ever belonged to the Tornabuoni family. Gombrich has also drawn attention to a possible similarity between the rôle of Venus, here leading the young man towards the liberal arts, and that of Venus of the *Primavera* (Plate 67) who acts as guide to *Humanitas* for the young Lorenzo di Pierfrancesco de' Medici. Since the dating of 1486 can be discounted if the frescoes were not made for the Albizi-Tornabuoni marriage, a dating on the basis of style can bring the picture earlier, nearer the time of the Sistine Chapel frescoes (Plates 36 and 31–38).

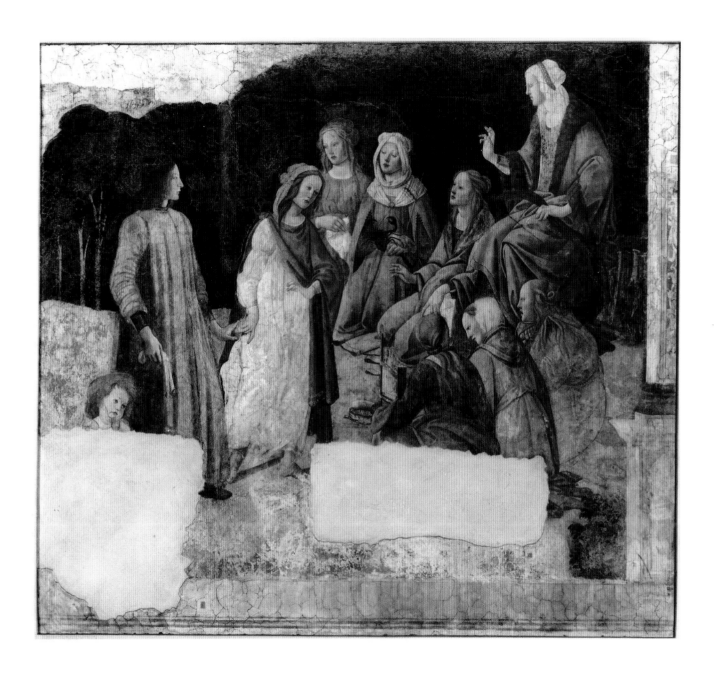

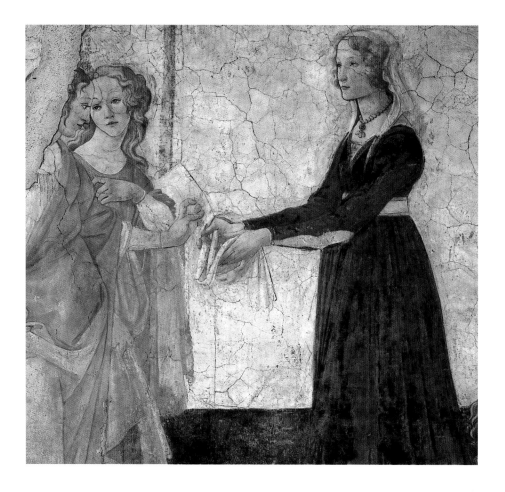

42 *Young Woman Receives Gifts*
PARIS, Musée du Louvre.
Fresco (detached) 212 x 284 cm.
Extensively damaged.

Like the *Young Man before the Liberal Arts* (Plate 41) this fresco, which has the same provenance, has suffered widespread damage and most of the *a secco* finishing is lost. The four figures to the left are usually identified as Venus, presenting a gift to the young woman, and the three Graces, but as with the first of the Villa Lemmi frescoes, the identification of the scene is far from clear.

(above)
Detail of *Young Women Recieves Gifts*

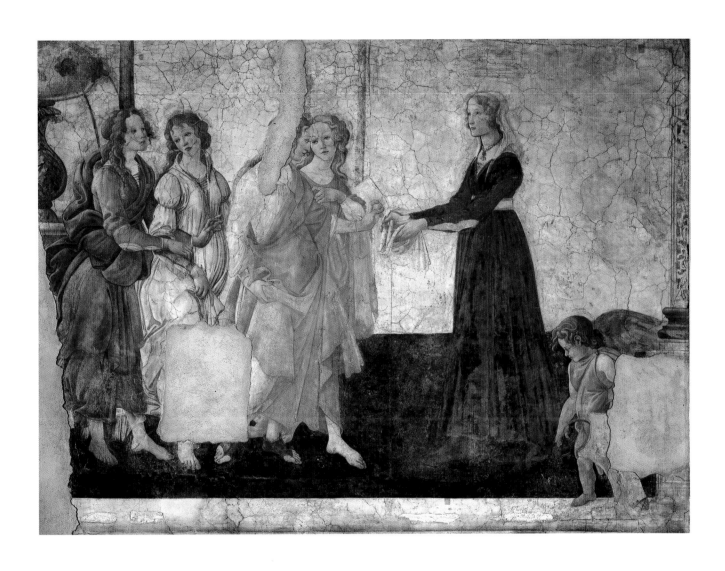

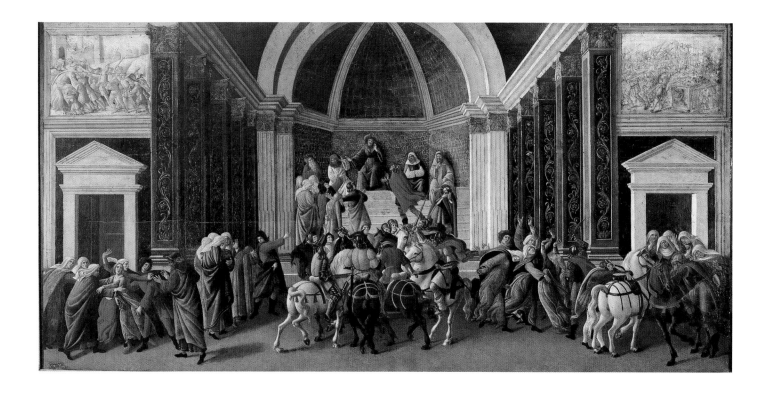

43 *The Story of Virginia*
BERGAMO, Accademia Carrara.
Tempera on panel 86 x 165 cm.

The Story of Virginia was purchased by Morelli at the
Monte di Pietà, Rome, and lent by him as by Botticelli to
an exhibition of Christian art in the Diocletian Baths in
1870. He bequeathed the picture to the Accademia
Carrara in 1891. The *Virginia* and *Lucretia* (Plate 44)
pictures are usually believed to be two elements in the
decorative series commissioned by a member of the
Vespucci family for their house in Via de' Servi. The
paintings were probably designed by Botticelli and
executed by his studio. Vasari reported, 'In Via de' Servi

in the house of Giovanni Vespucci, now that of Piero
Salviati, [Botticelli] painted round a room many pictures
containing numerous lively figures framed in walnut for
benchbacks and woodwork.' Guidantonio, not Giovanni,
Vespucci purchased the Via de' Servi house in March
1499, and so the two pictures cannot have been painted
before that date. *The Story of Virginia* is a legend of early
Rome told by Livy in Book III of his *History*. Virginius
kills his unfortunate daughter Virginia, to the right of the
picture, rather than let her fall into the hands of Appius
Claudius, in the centre, as his mistress or slave. The affair
is said to have led to a revolution in 449 B.C. Livy's *History*
was particularly admired by Dante.

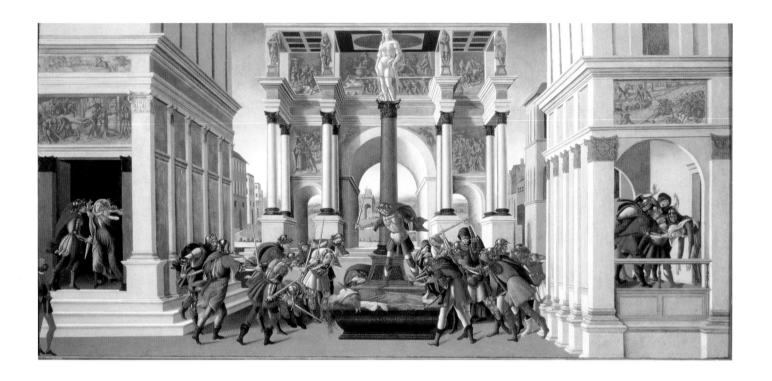

44 *The Story of Lucretia*

BOSTON, Isabella Stewart Gardner Museum.
Tempera on panel 83.5 x 180 cm.

Acquired by Mrs Gardner from the Earl of Ashburnham
through Bernard Berenson in 1894, this panel is thought
to have once decorated a room in the Vespucci home in
Via de'Servi, together with *The Story of Virginia* (Plate 41).
Lucretia, according to Livy's *History*, was raped by Sextus,
son of Tarquinius Superbus. Rather than face the ensuing
shame she kills herself (right).

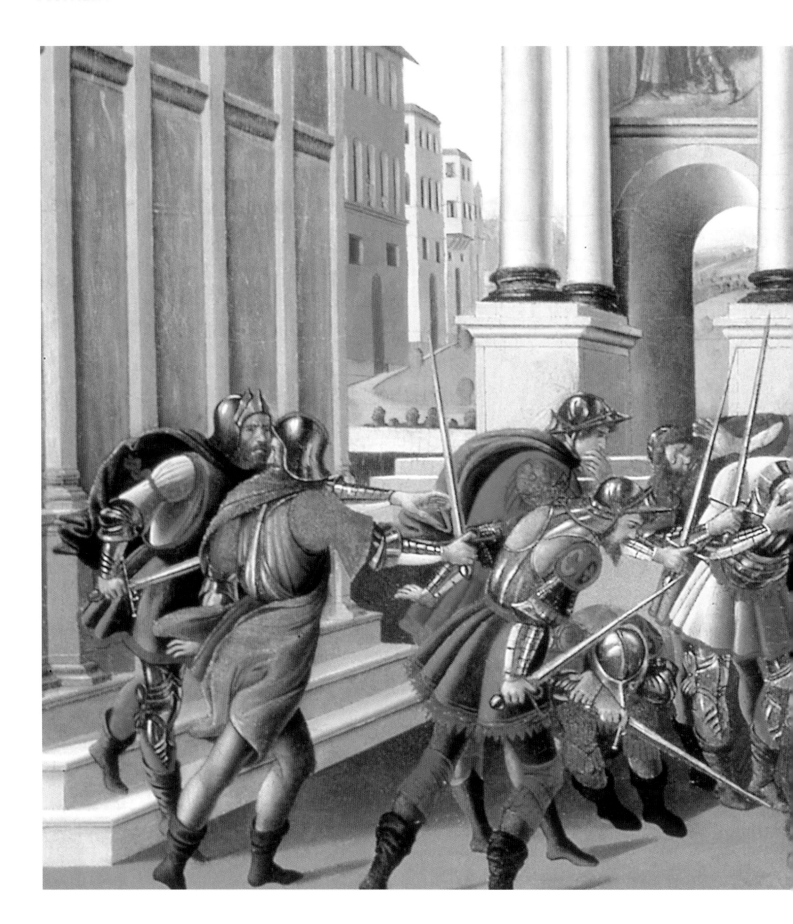

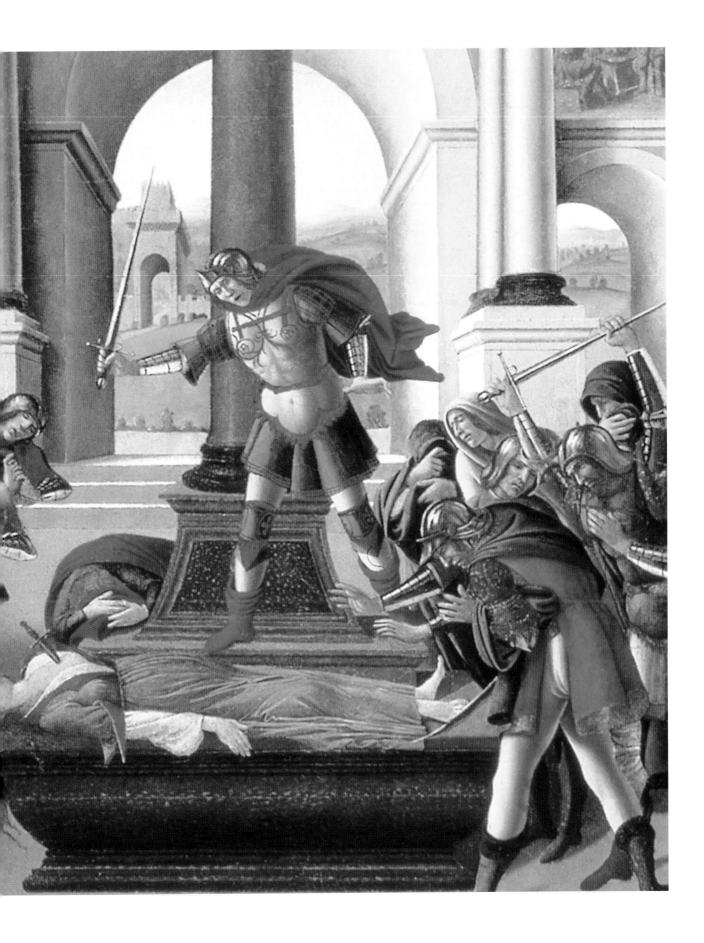

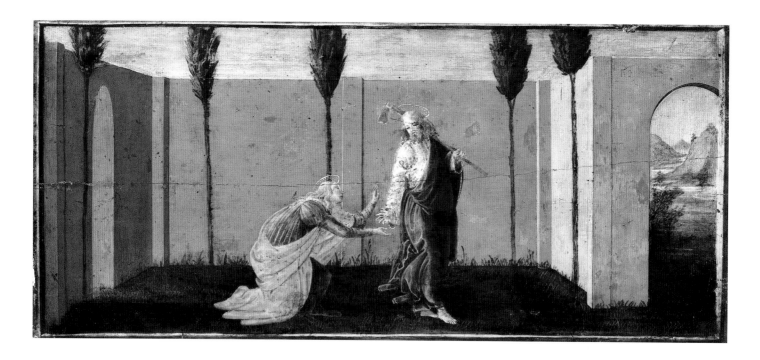

45 *The Risen Christ Appears to Mary Magdalen*
(*'Noli me Tangere'*)
PHILADELPHIA, Philadelphia Museum of Art (John G.
Johnson collection).
Tempera on panel 18.5 x 42.3 cm.

Four predella panels depicting the life of Mary Magdalen
survive in Philadelphia, *The Magdalen Listens to Christ
Preaching*, *The Magdalen Washes Christ's Feet*, this '*Noli me
Tangere*' and *The Magdalen's Communion and Ascension*. Horne
found the panels with the dealer Luigi Grassi in Florence,
and he recommended them to Johnson, believing them to
be the predella of the *Madonna and Child Enthroned with Six
Saints* (Plate 8) in the Uffizi. Roger Fry urged the
Metropolitan Museum, New York, to buy them but they
went to Johnson in 1908 for 160,000 lire. The lively
handling suggests a date later than the *Madonna and Child
Enthroned with Six Saints*, but it is not possible with present
knowledge to associate the predella with any known
altarpiece.

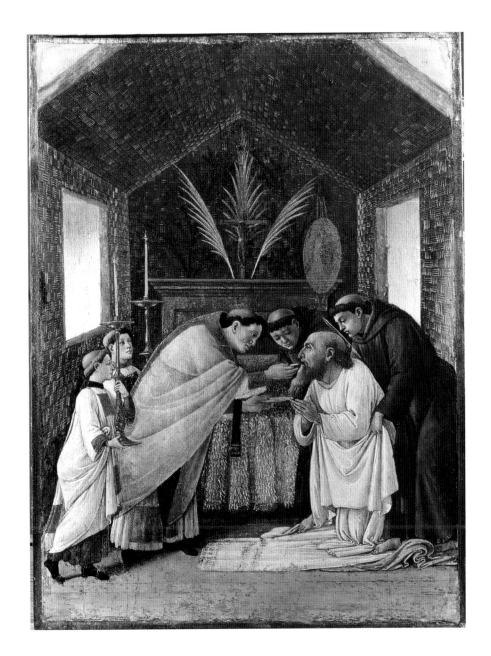

46 *The Communion of St Jerome*
NEW YORK, Metropolitan Museum of Art (bequest of
Benjamin Altman).
Tempera on panel 34.3 x 25.4 cm.

Another of Botticelli's smallest and most beautifully
painted pictures, *The Communion of St Jerome* is believed to
have been painted for Francesco di Filippo del Pugliese, a
wood-stapler and a follower of Savonarola. It was in the
collection of the Marchese Gino Capponi, Florence, by
1841 and was inherited by the Marchese Farinola who
sold it to Duveen, New York, in 1912. It was bequeathed
by Altman to the Metropolitan in the following year.
Botticelli's depiction of the last rites of the saint follows
Buonacorsi's *Life of St Jerome* published in Florence
in 1490.

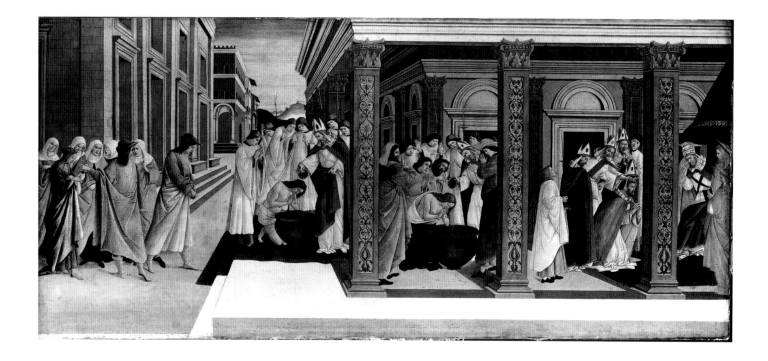

47 *Scenes from the Early Life of St Zenobius*
LONDON, National Gallery.
Tempera on panel 66.5 x 149.5 cm.

St Zenobius, Bishop of Florence, is little known outside
that city but scenes from his life have been depicted by a
large number of artists including Ghirlandaio, Gozzoli,
Veneziano and Ghiberti. The original home of Botticelli's
four pictures on this theme is unknown but they must
have formed a part of some decorative wall panelling
scheme. The majority of critics suggest a late date for the

group. The first set of scenes shows from the left,
Zenobius renouncing the bride chosen for him, Zenobius
being baptized by Theodosius, Bishop of Florence, the
baptism of his mother, his consecration as Bishop of
Florence by Pope St Damasus. The stories in each case
follow Tolosani's version of the legend, written in 1487.
All four panels were in the Rondinelli collection,
Florence, in the nineteenth century. This picture and the
Three Miracles of St Zenobius (Plate 48) were bought in 1891
for Dr Ludwig Mond by J. P. Richter. They were part of
the Mond bequest to the National Gallery in 1924.

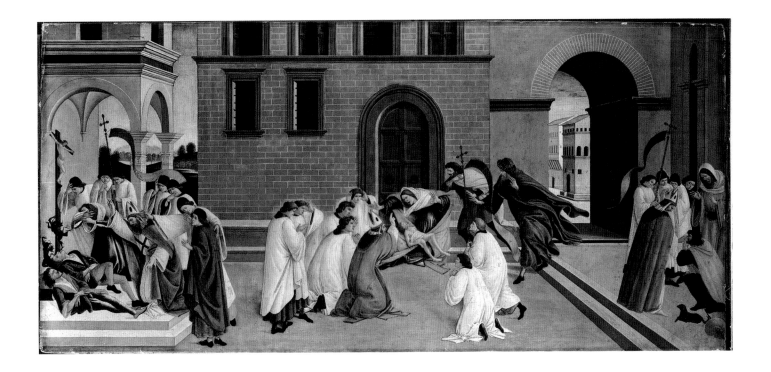

48 *Three Miracles of St Zenobius*
LONDON, National Gallery.
Tempera on panel 65 x 139.5 cm.

On the left Zenobius exorcizes two young men, in the
centre he restores to life a child who had died while left in
his care, and on the right he brings sight to a blind beggar.

The drawing of the figures is particularly vivid and fluent
and parallels for several of them can be found in the
illustrations to *La Divina Commedia* (Plates 71–74), though
not in the examples illustrated in this book. The
provenance for this picture is the same as that for the
Scenes from the Early Life of St Zenobius (Plate 47).

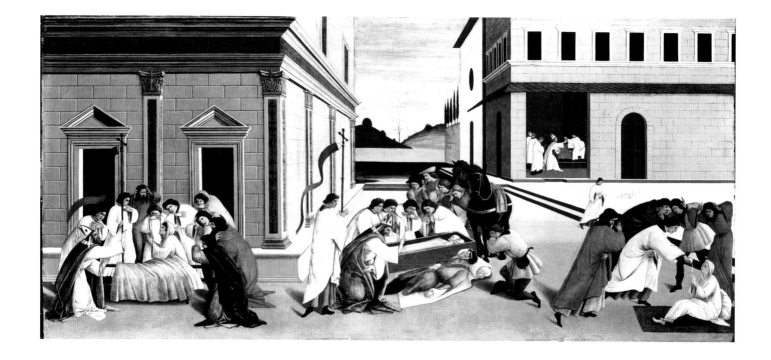

49 *Four Miracles of St Zenobius*
NEW YORK, Metropolitan Museum of Art
(Kennedy fund).
Tempera on panel 67.3 x 150.5 cm.

Restoration has revealed the coffin containing two
corpses, formerly overpainted.
Like the London panels, this picture of the *St Zenobius*
series was in the Rondinelli collection, Florence, in the
last century. It passed through the trade to Sir William
Abdy, London, by 1885 and was sold by him at Christie's
on 5 May 1911 to Langton Douglas. It was purchased by
the Metropolitan Museum of Art in the same year.
Zenobius on the left resuscitates one who had died, in the
centre raises a young man, in the background cures a sick
person and to the right empowers Deacon Eugenius to
revive a woman.

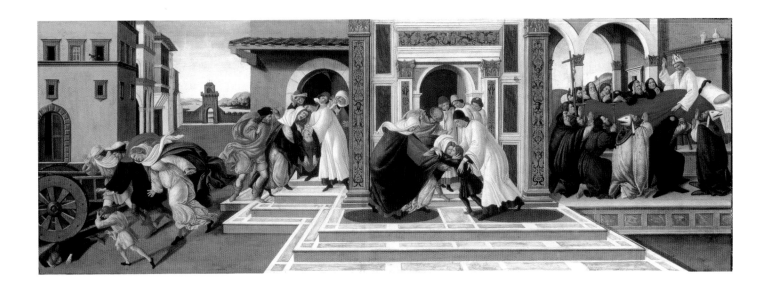

50 *The Last Acts of St Zenobius*
DRESDEN, Staatliche Gemäldegalerie.
Tempera on panel 66 x 182 cm.

A child run over by a cart on the left is carried to
Zenobius who revives him and restores him to his family.

Finally, from his bed, the saint announces his approaching
death. The panel went from the Rondinelli to the Metzger
collection. It entered the Gemäldegalerie from the von
Quandt collection in 1868.

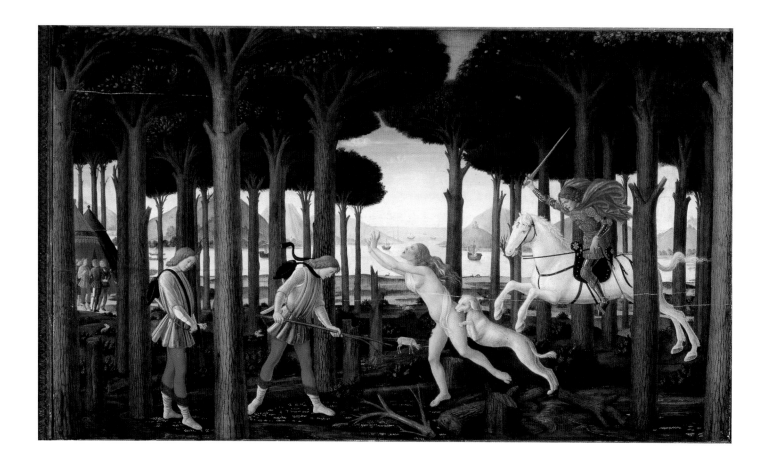

51 *The First Episode of the Story of Nastagio degli Onesti*
MADRID, Museo del Prado.
Tempera on panel 83 x 138 cm.

This panel is one of four scenes from the eighth tale of
the fifth day of Boccaccio's *Decameron*, the first three of
which are in the Prado, the fourth in an American private
collection. It seems likely that the scenes were designed by
Botticelli but executed by his studio. Vasari mentioned the
four panels as being in the house of the Pucci family,
Florence (see map, pp. 24–25), and Horne suggested that
they were painted at the time of the wedding of
Giannozzo Pucci and Lucrezia Bini in 1483. They
remained with the Pucci until 1868 when they were sold
to Barker, London and from there passed to Leyland;
Aynard (1892); Spiridon, Paris; Cambo, Barcelona and the

Prado. The fourth panel, after leaving Aynard went to
Donaldson and then the Watney collection, Charlbury. Sir
Charles Eastlake, who saw all four pictures at the Casa
Pucci, calls the story 'repulsive' in his first notebook of
1861. Nastagio, in despair at being rejected by the
daughter of Paolo Traversaro, wanders brooding on his
ill-fortune through a pinewood at Chiassi, near Ravenna.
Suddenly he encounters an apparition of a naked young
woman being chased by dogs and a knight who, catching
her, cuts out her heart and feeds it to the dogs. On
hearing the story the young Traversaro girl, through fear
of suffering a similar fate, bows to the wishes of
Nastagio, and, recounted Boccaccio, ladies of Ravenna 'all
became, and have ever since been, much more compliant
with men's desires than they were wont to be'.

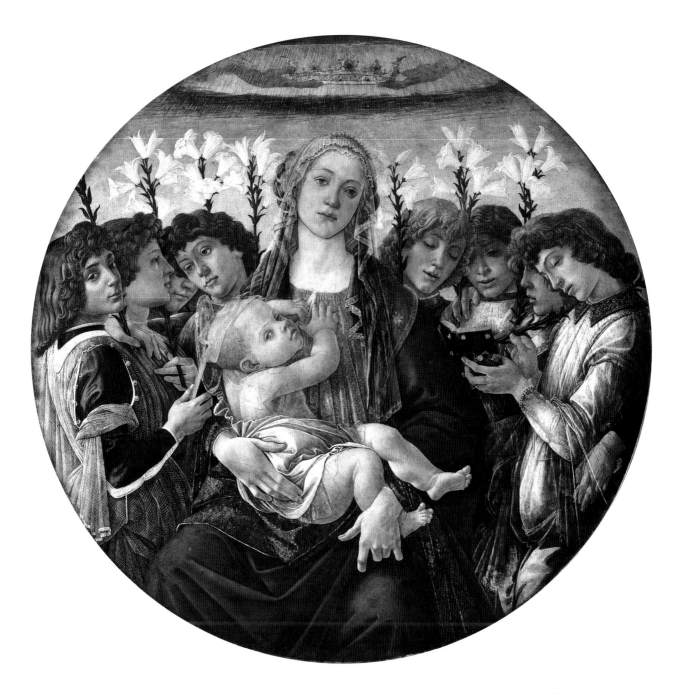

52 *The Raczinsky Tondo*
BERLIN Gemäldegalerie.
Tempera on panel 135 cm. diameter.
Damaged; extensive retouching.

The picture was brought to Paris as Napoleonic booty and
purchased there in 1824 by Count Raczinsky of Berlin, passing
from him to the Staatliche Gemäldegalerie. It is usually identified
with the tondo described by Vasari in the Church of San Francesco
outside Porta San Miniato, now known as San Salvatore al Monte
(see map, pp. 24–25). Francesco Bocchi in *Le Bellezze di Firenze*
(1591) also recorded in the same church, 'In a chapel on the right
hand side one sees a very beautiful tondo by Sandro Botticelli',
which, he added, was particularly admired by craftsmen: 'E stimata

molto questa pittura da gli Artefici'. The lily, which plays an
important rôle in the composition of this tondo, is symbolic of
virginity and purity and as such is often associated with the
Madonna in Annunciations (Plates 58, 59 and 60) and other
devotional pictures, such as *The Bardi Altarpiece* (Plate 9). If the
usual dating of 1475–80 is accepted the picture cannot originally
have been made for a site in the Church of San Salvatore which
stands today, as the Franciscans only began work on the church in
1487. The circular Madonna and Child theme was more often
found in a domestic setting or private chapel than in a church, but
this picture must have looked well in its adoptive home, San
Salvatore being a Florentine building of unusual warmth, fondly
called by Michelangelo 'the pretty country lass'.

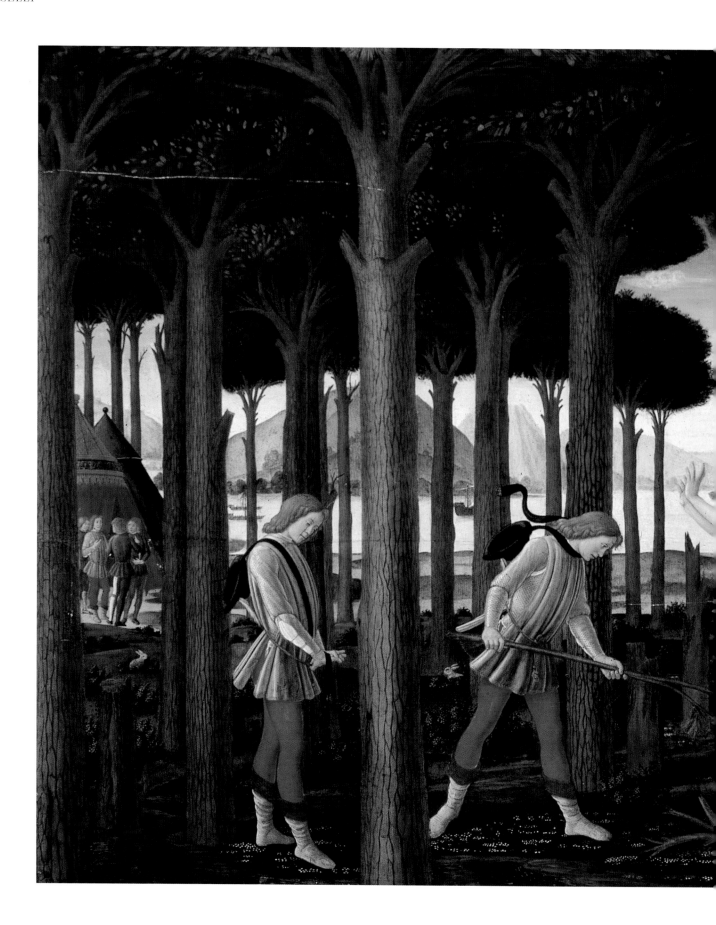

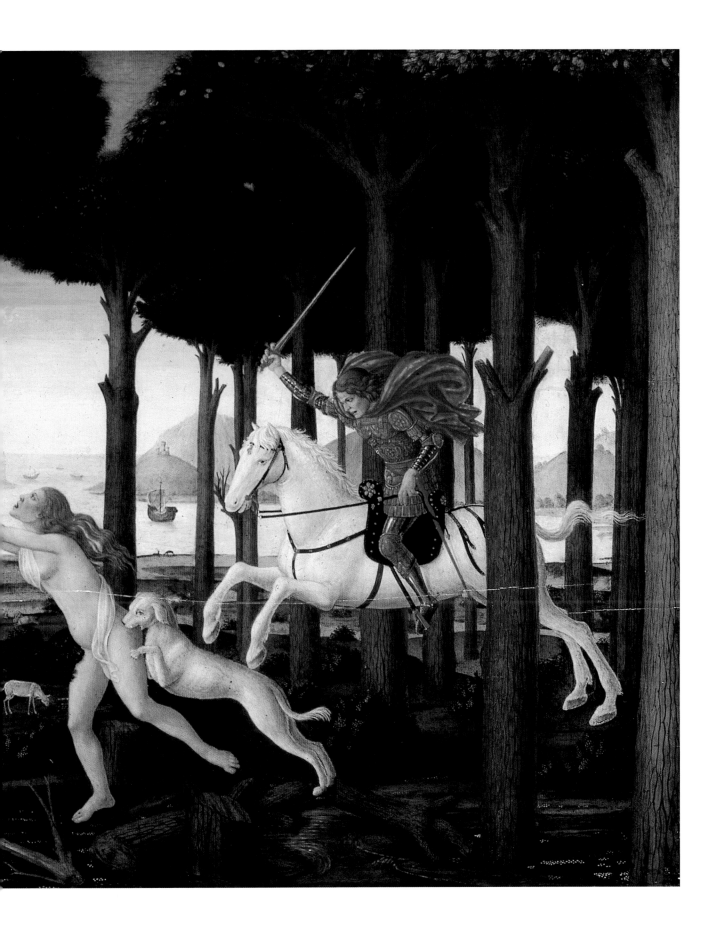

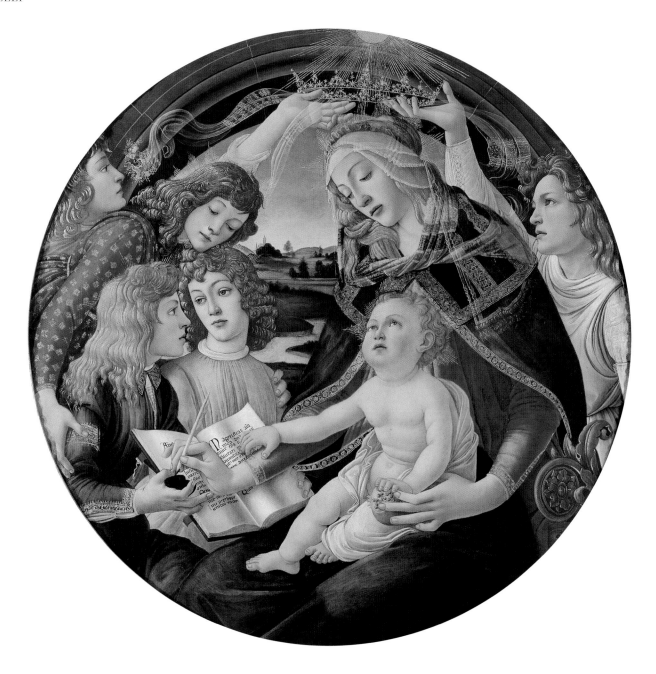

53 *Madonna of the Magnificat*
FLORENCE, Galleria degli Uffizi. Tempera on panel
118 cm. diameter. Damage and retouching on the faces of
the Madonna and the Christ Child.

John Addington Symonds in 1877 called this Botticelli's
'best known picture'. He believed it combined 'all
Botticelli's best qualities. For rare distinction of beauty in
the faces it is unique, while the mystic calm and
resignation, so misplaced in his Aphrodites, find a
meaning here'. The picture was acquired by the Uffizi as
an anonymous work in 1784 from Ottavio Margherini
and attributed to Botticelli in the nineteenth century,
probably first by Cavalcaselle in 1864. The Madonna is
shown writing the Magnificat (Luke I, 46–55), while
being crowned by angels. The picture is usually dated in
the 1480s, and the highly polished technique renders it
comparable with *The Bardi Altarpiece* (Plate 9) of 1484–85.
It has frequently suffered from being reproduced at an
angle without a proper regard for the lines of the distant
landscape. A number of variant copies exist.

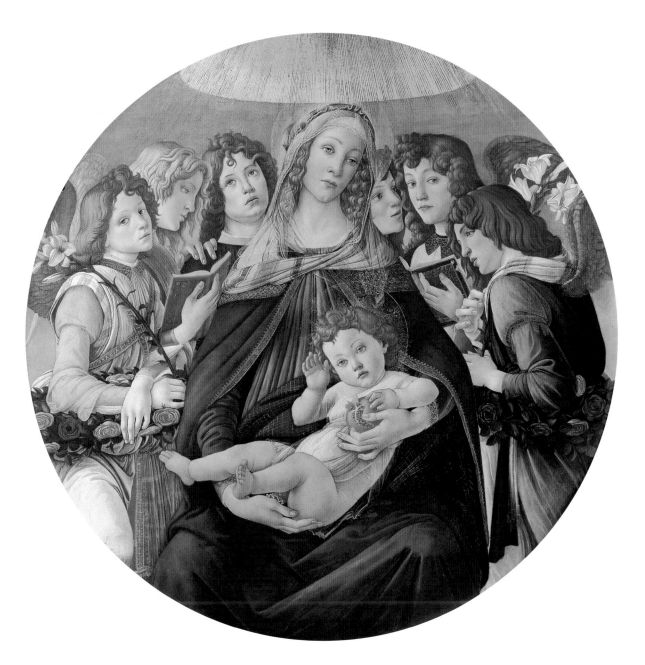

54 *Madonna of the Pomegranate*
FLORENCE, Galleria degli Uffizi.
Tempera on panel 143.5 cm. diameter.

Although the design of this tondo of the mid-1480s is a restatement of the composition of *The Raczinsky Tondo* (Plate 52), certain telling details such as the hands of the Madonna, which in the earlier picture were thin and angular, have changed fundamentally with the maturing of the artist's style. The angels have graduated from a rather indolent human crowd to a more heavenly winged group who actively contribute to the tondo composition by pressing in on the Madonna and Child instead of leaning out against the circumference of the panel as they did in *The Raczinsky Tondo*. The pomegranate, also used by Botticelli in his early *Madonna and Child in an Archway* (Plate 2) and in the *Madonna of the Magnificat* (Plate 53), is an ancient Semitic symbol of fertility and regeneration sometimes translated into a Christian image of immortality. The picture was listed in 1675 among the possessions of Cardinal Leopoldo de' Medici, from whom it went to the Medici grand dukes and then to the Uffizi in 1780. It may have been the tondo painted for the audience chamber of the Magistrato de' Massai della Camera in the Palazzo della Signoria in 1487.

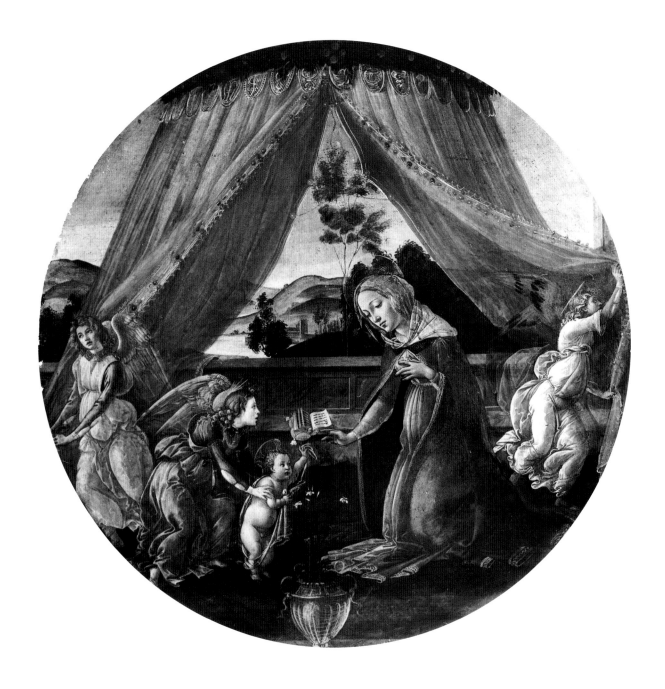

55 *Madonna and Child with Three Angels*
MILAN, Pinacoteca Ambrosiana.
Tempera on panel 65 cm. diameter.

It is possible that this, much the smallest of Botticelli's
tondo pictures, was the one seen by Vasari in the
Monastery of Santa Maria degli Angeli in Via degli Alfani
(see map, pp. 24–25) which was suppressed in 1808. Even
if it were not this picture it would admirably fit Vasari's
description of a painting 'made with beautiful care'. It has
always been accepted as a late work of the 1490s.

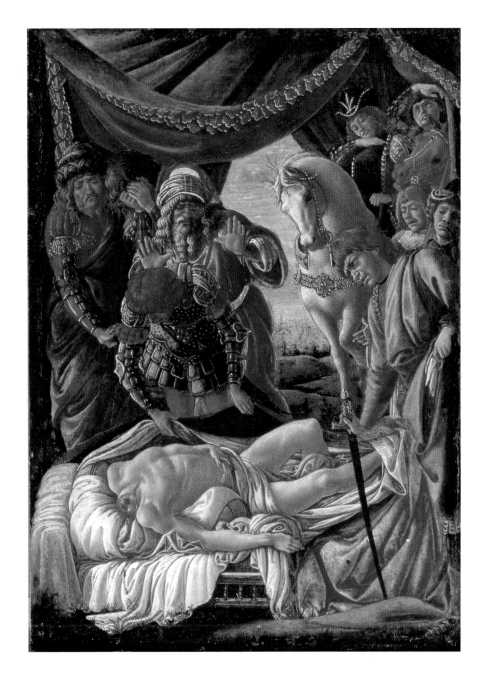

56 *The Finding of the Dead Holofernes*
FLORENCE, Galleria degli Uffizi.
Tempera on panel 31 x 25 cm.

The picture probably formed a diptych with *The Return of Judith* (Plate 57). They were given by Rodolfo Sirigatti to Bianca Cappello, second wife of the Grand Duke Francesco I de' Medici around 1580. Her son Antonio inherited them and at his death in 1632 the panels went to the Uffizi. Judith, a young widow from Bethulia, a town besieged by the Babylonians, deceived Holofernes the Babylonian general into believing her to be an ally. Every night she crossed the siege lines to visit his tent until one night his drunken sleep gave her the opportunity to murder him and thus secure the collapse of the siege. Judging from the figure types the pictures must date from the period of the two early *Adoration* pictures in the National Gallery, London (Plates 17 and 19): the man to the back on the right in this picture who looks upward and raises his arm to shield the light from his eyes has a parallel in the figure on the extreme left of the rectangular London *Adoration* (Plate 17). The body of Holofernes is Botticelli's earliest known attempt at portraying a male nude. A more accomplished rendering of the male torso can be seen in the *Venus and Mars* (Plate 62) and the Munich *Pietà* (Plate 61).

57 *The Return of Judith*
FLORENCE, Galleria degli Uffizi.
Tempera on panel 31 x 24 cm.

The delicate grey and chalky blue colour scheme of
Judith's dress helps to make this the prettiest of
Botticelli's early pictures, despite the gruesome subject
matter. The foot of Judith was originally painted further
to the right. It was probably altered by Botticelli so that

the line of her leg should not echo exactly that of the
forward stepping leg of the maid. Judith carries an olive
branch very similar to those held by figures in *The Mystic
Nativity* (Plate 21). The branch was presumably intended
to signify that Judith, on her return to Bethulia with the
Head of Holofernes, was bringing peace to the city.
Another small panel of *Judith with the Head of Holofernes* by
Botticelli is in the Rijksmuseum, Amsterdam. It has been
cut down and is very damaged.

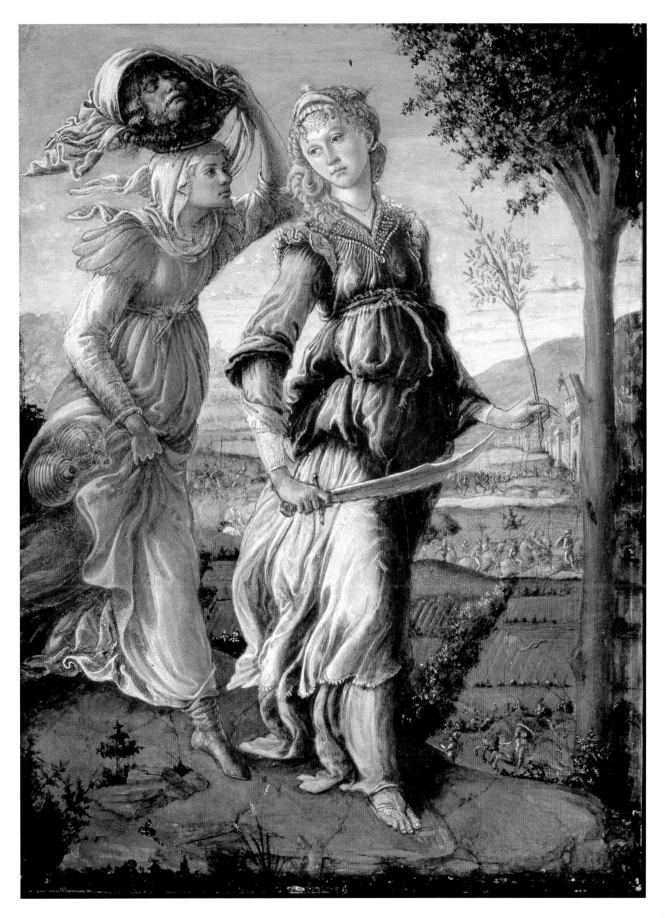

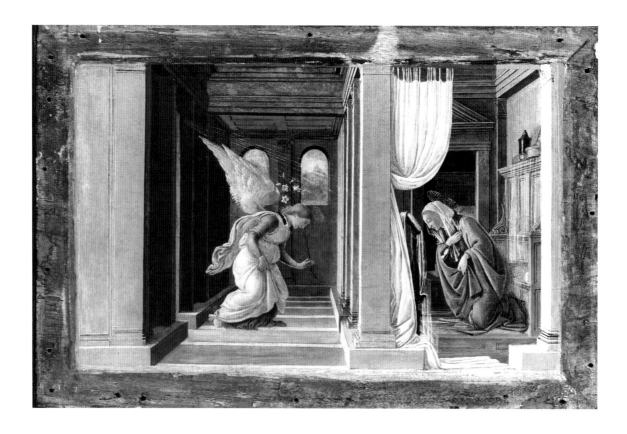

58 *The Annunciation*
NEW YORK, Metropolitan Museum of Art
(Robert Lehman collection).
Tempera on panel 24 x 36 cm.

This small *Annunciation* was given with the Lehman
collection to the Metropolitan Museum in 1969.
Previously it had belonged to Huldschinsky of Berlin and
the Barberini collection, Rome. Its earlier history is
unknown. Despite the grandeur of the architecture the
scene is realized as an intimate domestic interior. The
curtain serves a similar function to the one in the *St
Augustine in his Cell* (Plate 37), a picture of about the same

size. Suggestions for dating the picture differ very greatly.
All that can be said with a degree of certainty is that it
must be before the Glasgow *Annunciation* (Plate 60),
which dates from around 1500. By comparison with the
Glasgow picture the architecture is rather cramped and
the figures lacking in grace and balance. In the Lehman
Annunciation the wings of the angel are rather awkwardly
made to follow the lines of the rays representing the
entrance of the Holy Spirit, with the result that the angel
appears to be toppling forward and looking at the floor
rather than towards the Virgin. No such problems exist in
the Glasgow picture.

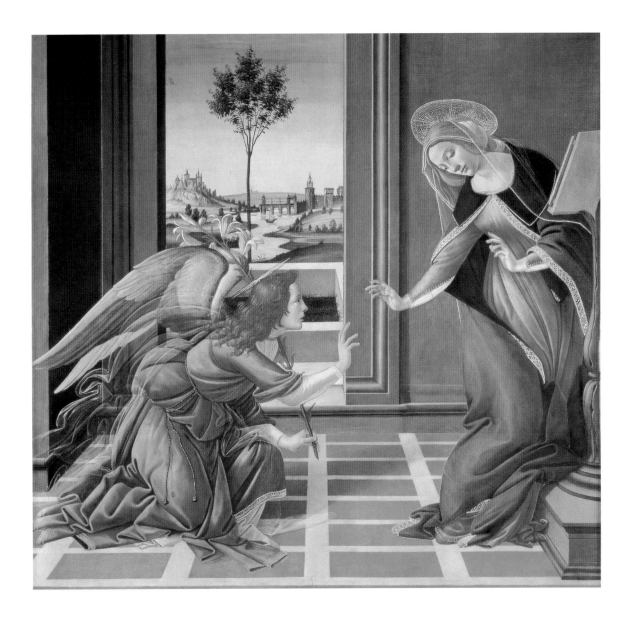

59 *The Annunciation*

FLORENCE, Galleria degli Uffizi.
Tempera on panel 150 x 156 cm.

This picture was made for the chapel of Benedetto Guardi, the second from the right in the Church of Santa Maria Maddelena de' Pazzi in Florence. According to the *libro de' benefattori* of the church, quoted by Horne, the chapel was built between March 1489 and June 1490, and the altarpiece which was made during this period cost thirty ducats. The empty room in which the scene takes place and the landscape background differ very greatly from the architectural settings of the Lehman and Glasgow pictures and appear to reflect a knowledge of Flemish models. The rather stiff and dry handling of the picture led Horne to the conclusion that it was a studio work. Although it may have been in part painted by studio hands the conception must have been Botticelli's and a similar style can be seen in the two *Pietà* pictures (Plates 61 and 63) and the *Pentecost* (Plate 64). This rather bland manner in which the artist occasionally worked is hard to characterize, but if the Uffizi *Annunciation* is compared with a picture on a similar scale, such as *The Bardi Altarpiece* (Plate 9), it can be seen that *The Annunciation* suffers from a dearth of ornamentation both in costumes and the setting. *The Annunciation* was found in 1870 in a chapel near Fiesole belonging to the nuns of Santa Maria Maddelena de' Pazzi and was taken to the Uffizi in 1872.

60 *The Annunciation*

GLASGOW, City Art Gallery and Museum.
Tempera on panel 51 x 61 cm., including
narrow strips added at top and bottom.
Extensive retouching.

The provenance of this, the latest of
Botticelli's Annunciations has recently been
traced by Martin Kemp. From the evidence
of an old inscription on the back of the panel
he has shown that the picture was originally
in the Church of San Barnaba, Florence,
which also housed *The San Barnaba Altarpiece*
(Plate 10). The picture was purchased in the
early 1830s by the Revd. John Sandford from
the Casa Rivani in Florence and sold in 1839
to a 'Davis' for £4 12s. It subsequently
entered the collection of Archibald McLellan
of Glasgow and then in 1856, two years after
his death, became the property of the
Glasgow Corporation. The picture was on
public view in the McLellan Galleries,
Glasgow from 1855 to 1902, when it was
moved to its present home. Like *The Agony in
the Garden* (Plate 25) it has suffered a lack of
serious recognition because of its somewhat
out of the way location. When seen in the
original the high quality of the picture is
apparent despite its unhappy condition. It is
equal in intensity of expression to works such
as the Dante drawings and *The Mystic Nativity*
(Plate 21). As in the Dante illustrations the
setting plays a part in the narrative. As Martin
Kemp has observed, Botticelli actually moved
the lines of the architecture out of
perpendicular during the course of painting
in order to emphasize the narrative flow of
the subject. The central column, for example,
inclines towards the entrance of the angel on
the left. Botticelli's versions of the
Annunciation illustrated here do not form a
coherent group in the way that, for instance,
the Adoration pictures do, mainly because the
Uffizi *Annunciation* (Plate 59) has such an
entirely different kind of setting from the
other two and is also a great deal larger in
scale.

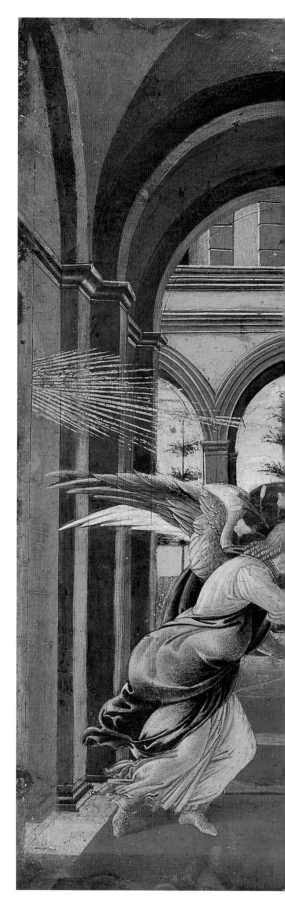

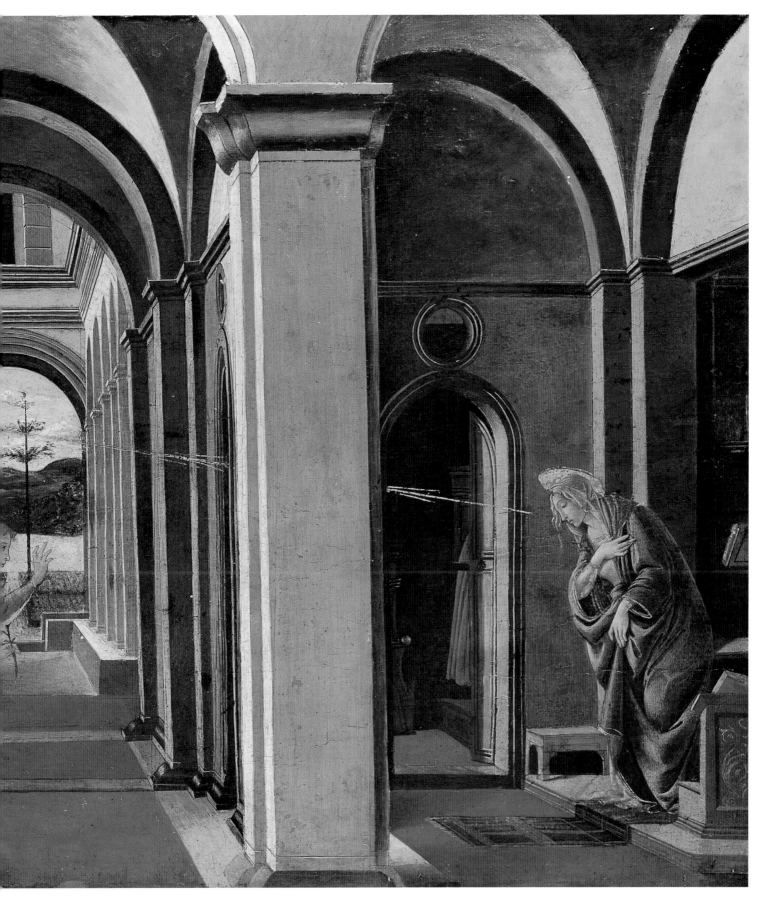

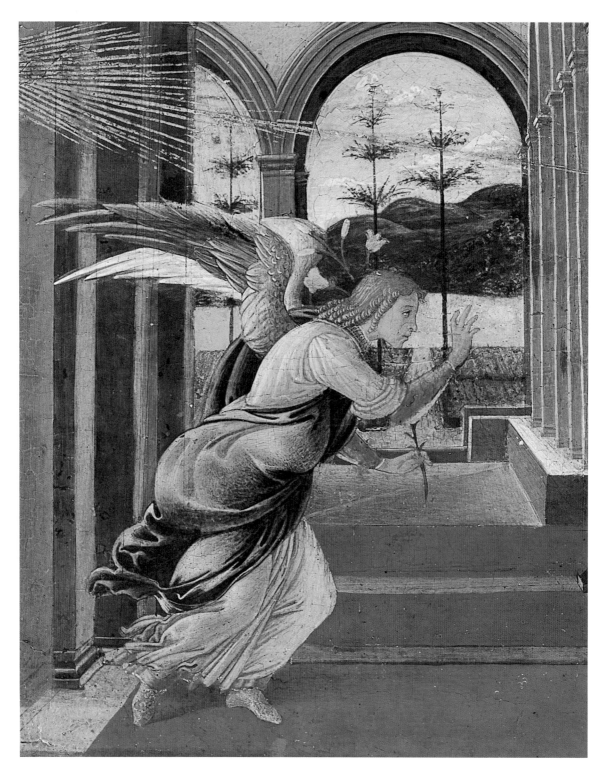

Detail of The Annunication (Plate 60)

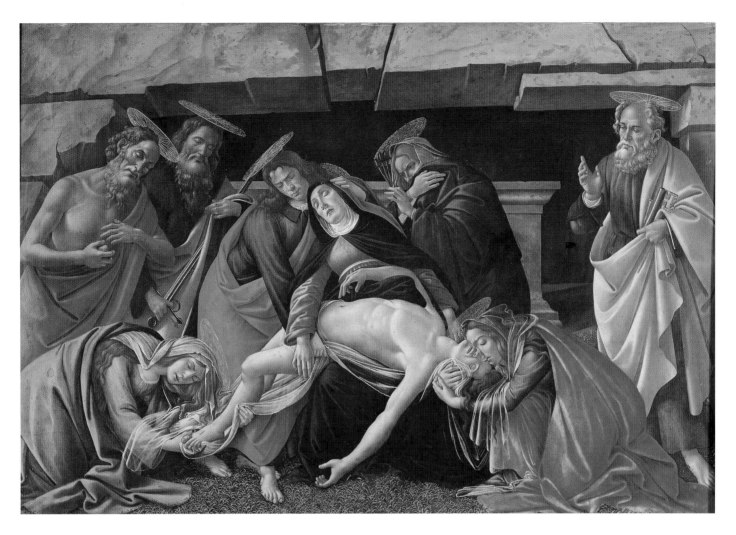

61 *Pietà*

MUNICH, Alte Pinakothek.
Tempera on panel 139.5 x 207.3 cm.

The picture was bought by Crown Prince Ludwig of
Bavaria, later Ludwig I, in 1814 from the Church of San
Paolino very near Botticelli's home in Florence (see map,
pp. 24–25). It passed into the possession of the Bavarian
state in 1850, and although it has hung as a Botticelli in
the Alte Pinakothek since 1836 a number of scholars
have questioned the extent of Botticelli's participation. To
the eye accustomed to the decorative appeal of such
popular pictures as the *Madonna of the Magnificat* (Plate 53),
the rather bland areas of colour are somewhat

disconcerting but the artist employed a rather similar style
in several other pictures of his later period, notably in the
Birmingham *Pentecost* (Plate 64) and the Uffizi *Annunciation*
(Plate 59) commissioned in 1489. In the case of the *Pietà*
he could well have considered a plainer style to be in
sympathy with the subject. The pathos of the scene is
heightened by the contrast between the pale, youthful
body and beardless face of Christ and the rugged figures
of the three older saints who look on. The Christ is very
close to the Mars of *Venus and Mars* (Plate 62) in the
National Gallery, London. The picture probably dates
from the early 1490s, less than a decade before
Michelangelo's St Peter's *Pietà*.

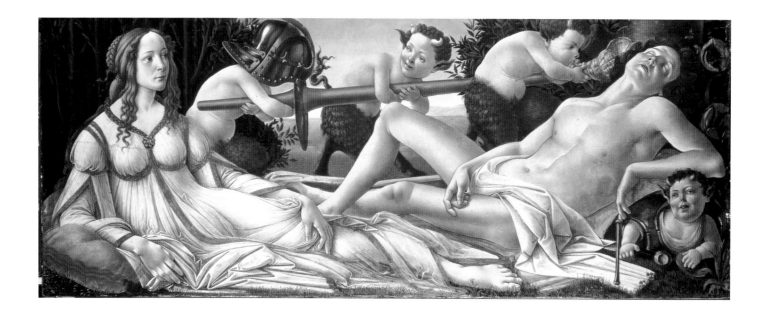

62 *Venus and Mars*
LONDON, National Gallery.
Tempera on panel 69 x 173.5 cm.

Botticelli's only major mythological picture to be found outside Italy, *Venus and Mars* was purchased between 1864 and 1869 by Alexander Barker in Florence and bought by the National Gallery at the Barker sale in 1874. There is no record of its earlier provenance, but Gombrich has suggested that the wasps (*vespe*) near Mars's head may refer to the Vespucci family by whom Botticelli is known to have been employed (cf. Plates 43 and 44). There can be no definitive analysis of the subject, but it appears to be Love, personified by Venus, transcending War, Mars, asleep and disarmed by satyrs. The picture must date from the mid to late 1480s. The Venus is very close in type to the St Catherine of *The San Barnaba Altarpiece* (Plate 10) of 1488–90. John Addington Symonds harboured an irrational dislike for the picture and for Mars in particular: 'The face and attitude of that unseductive Venus . . . opposite her snoring lover, seems to symbolise the indignities which women have to endure from insolent and sottish boys with only youth to recommend them.'

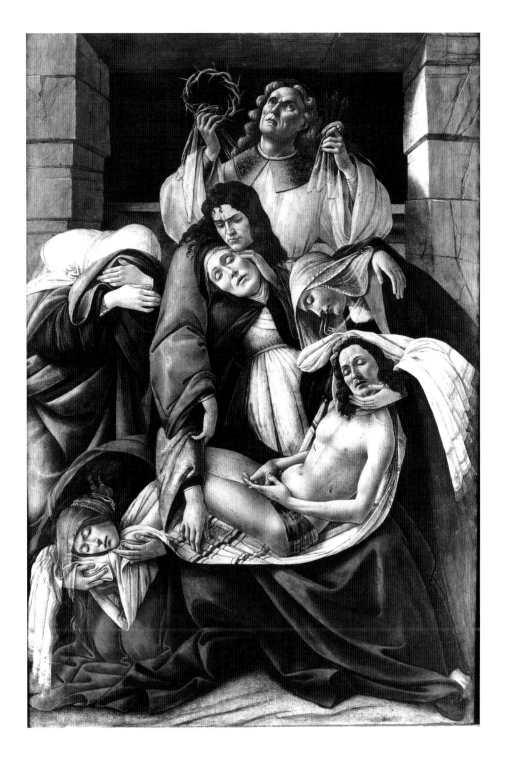

63 *The Panciatichi Pietà*

MILAN, Museo Poldi-Pezzoli.
Tempera on panel 107 x 71 cm. Restored 1951; extensive overpainting removed.

Like the early *St Sebastian* (Plate 7) this panel hung on one of the pillars in Santa Maria Maggiore. Vasari mentioned it in the second edition of his *Vite* (1568), 'at the side of the Chapel of the Panciatichi' ('allato capella di Panciatichi'). The picture was in the sacristy by 1755. The Museo Poldi-Pezzoli acquired it from the antiquarian Baslini in 1855. Only since restoration has it emerged as an undoubted autograph work of Botticelli related in style and probably in date to the Munich *Pietà* (Plate 61). A bad copy in the Bautier collection, Brussels, has sometimes mistakenly been associated with Botticelli's studio.

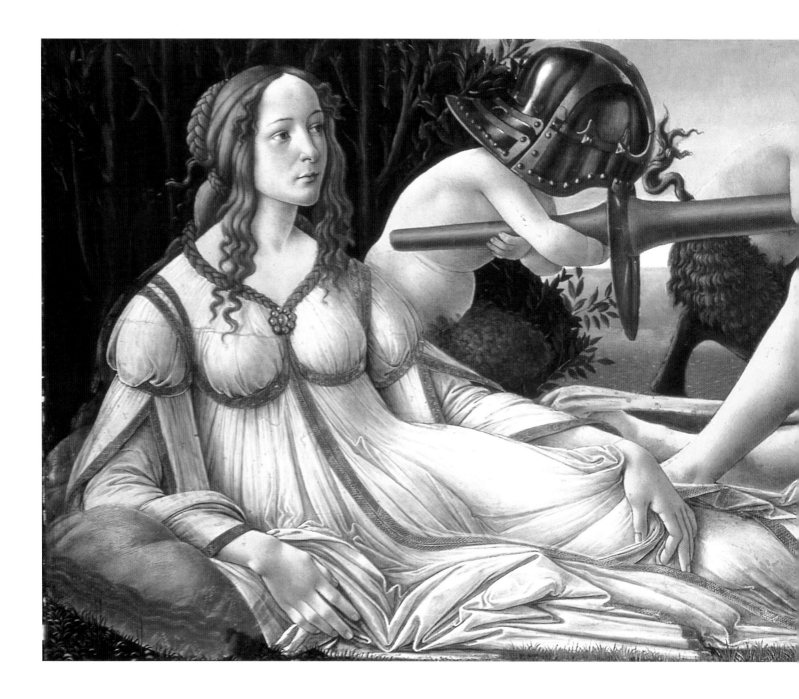

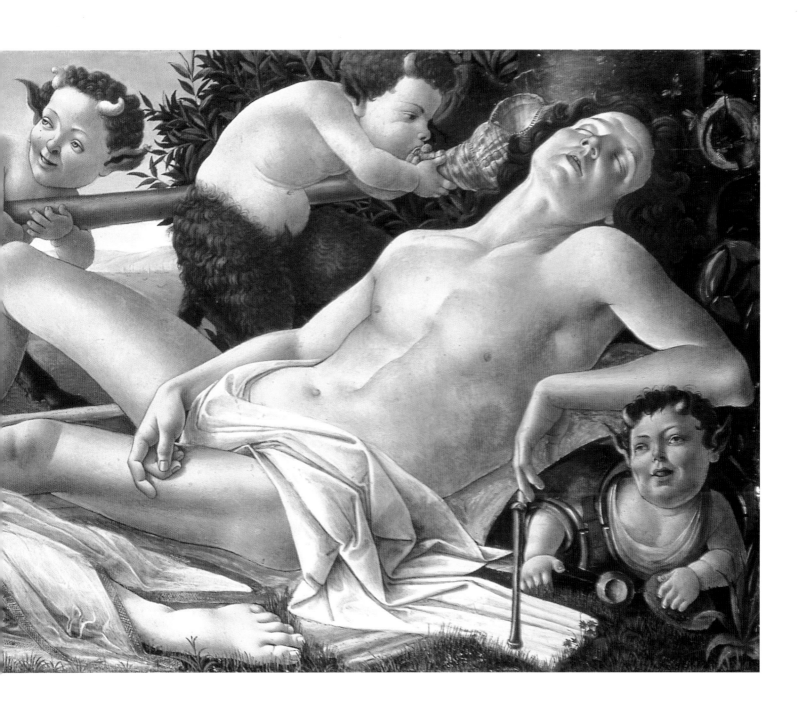

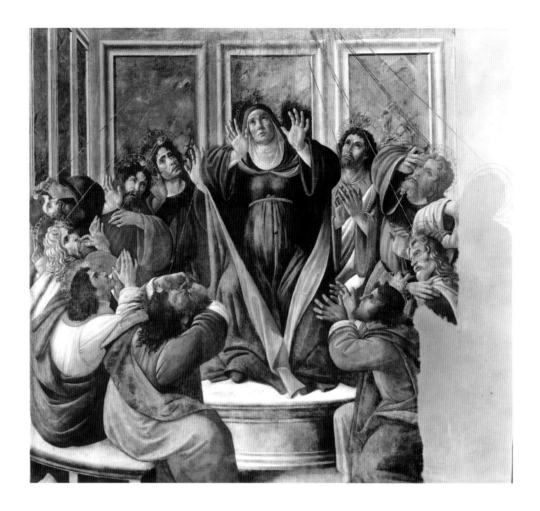

64 Pentecost
BIRMINGHAM, City Art Gallery.
Tempera on panel 221 x 229 cm.
 Numerous losses and old retouchings; restored 1973.

The picture was purchased by Birmingham in 1959 from Julius Weitzner after an export licence had been refused to Bob Jones University, Greenville, South Carolina. Mandel and Salvini mistakenly catalogue it as at Greenville. Earlier the *Pentecost* had been in the Cook collection, Richmond and immediately before that, until 1874, with the Abbé Hyeres at the Jesuit College, Lyons. He had purchased it in 1872 from Michele and Luigi Gamberini who believed it to be *The Convertite Altarpiece* (cf. Plate 8). The subject is from Acts II, 1–4: 'they were all together in one place. And suddenly a sound came from heaven like the rush of a mighty wind, and it filled all the house where they were sitting. And there appeared to them tongues as of fire, distributed and resting on each one of them. And they were all filled with the Holy Spirit . . .' Cannon-Brookes has pointed out that the composition follows a type usually found in miniatures. The subject is rarely found on any larger scale but the great round window of Santo Spirito is decorated with a *Pentecost* designed by Perugino in about 1500. In Perugino's composition the Apostles are similarly grouped in a circle round the Virgin, but they are standing rather than seated. Botticelli's picture is probably slightly earlier than the window design, dating from the period between the Munich and the Panciatichi *Pietàs* (Plates 61 and 63) and *The Mystic Nativity* (Plate 21).

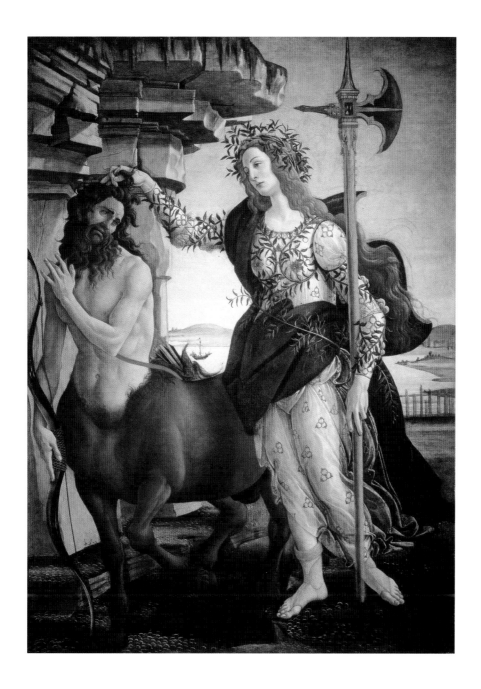

65 *Pallas and the Centaur*
FLORENCE, Galleria degli Uffizi.
Tempera on canvas 207 x 148 cm.
Probably transferred from panel.

This picture has had a chequered history. It was once at Castello in the collection of Lorenzo and Giovanni di Pierfrancesco de' Medici and then in that of Giovanni 'delle Bande Nere' de' Medici. It was still at Castello in 1638 but went to the Palazzo Pitti around 1830. It was 'rediscovered' in about 1893 in, according to Julia Cartwright, 'a dark corner of the Pitti Palace', and moved to the Uffizi. Its appearance is marred today by the presence of numerous faded retouchings covering most areas of the canvas. The dress of Pallas is decorated with the personal badge of Lorenzo 'il Magnifico'. Several political interpretations of the picture have been proposed but latterly scholars have preferred to see it as related to Marsilio Ficino's concept of the duality of the soul, half-animal and sensual and half-human and capable of reason. Pallas Athena or Minerva, Wisdom, guides or restrains the centaur, a creature of visibly dual nature.

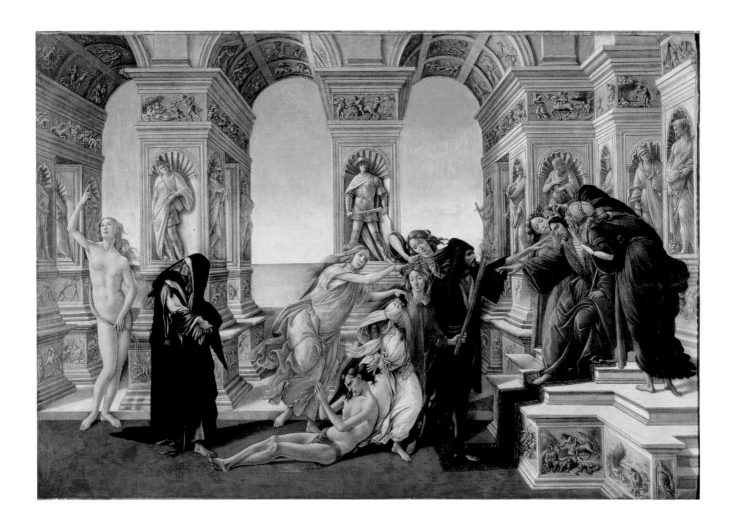

66 The 'Calumny' of Apelles
FLORENCE, Galleria degli Uffizi.
Tempera on panel 62 x 91 cm.

Lucian, the Greek writer of the second century A.D., described in detail the *Calumny* painted by his compatriot Apelles in the fourth century B.C. Apelles was the official painter to the Macedonian court and reputedly the only man allowed to portray Alexander the Great. Alberti paraphrased Lucian's description in his *De Pictura*, Book III, paragraph 53, thus: 'In the painting there was a man with enormous ears sticking out, attended on each side by two women, Ignorance and Suspicion; from one side Calumny was approaching in the form of an attractive woman, but whose face seemed too well versed in cunning, and she was holding in her left hand a lighted torch, while with her right she was dragging by the hair a youth with his arms outstretched towards heaven. Leading her was another man, pale, ugly and fierce to look upon, whom you would rightly compare to those

exhausted by long service in the field. They identified him correctly as Envy. There are two other women attendant on Calumny and busy arranging their mistress's dress; they are Treachery and Deceit. Behind comes Repentance clad in mourning and rending her hair, and in her train chaste and modest Truth.' The sculptural setting in Botticelli's painting was probably intended to evoke the spirit of a classical age, but the figures and reliefs do not relate stylistically to known classical pieces, and they represent a miscellany of subjects both Christian and mythological. The figure of St George in the niche on the central column appears to be derived from Andrea Castagno's *Pippo Spano* fresco in Sant' Apollonia, Florence. The figure of 'Modest Truth' on the left, like the Venus of *The Birth of Venus* (Plate 68), is related to the classical sculpture *Venus Pudica*. Proposals for dating this picture vary between 1485 and 1495. It was presented by Botticelli to Antonio Segni of Florence, according to Vasari, who saw it in his son Fabio Segni's house. It passed to the Pitti and then in 1773 to the Uffizi.

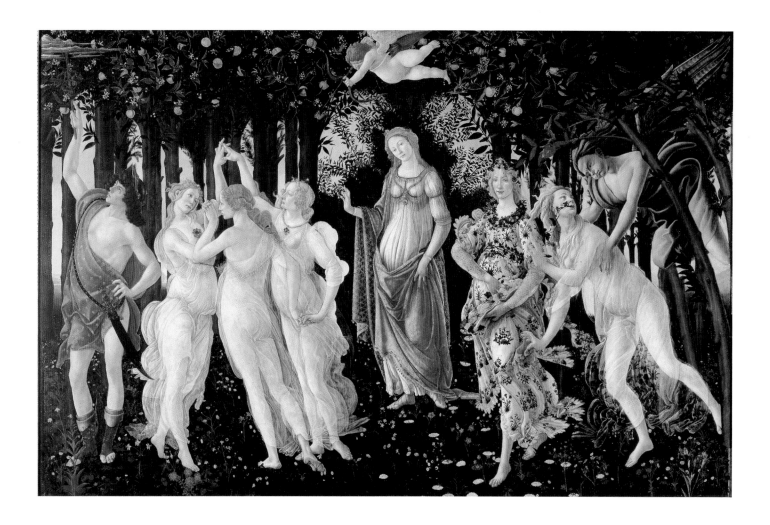

67 *Primavera (Spring)*
FLORENCE, Galleria degli Uffizi.
Tempera on panel 203 x 314 cm.

Lorenzo di Pierfrancesco de' Medici, who inherited a
fortune at the death of his father Pierfrancesco in 1476,
acquired the Villa di Castello in 1477 and may have had
the *Primavera* executed for this, his country home, in the
following year. Interpretations of the subject of the
picture are legion. Vasari rather inaccurately calls it 'a
Venus, whom the Graces are covering with flowers ["lo
fioriscono"] denoting spring'. As in two of the Sistine
frescoes the theme (it can hardly be called narrative) reads
from right to left. The impetus is given by Zephyr who
blows from the right. On the left, Mercury, assocaited

with the month of May, turns as if to indicate the passage
of spring towards summer. Zephyr's breath causes
flowers to spring from the mouth of the earth nymph
Chloris, who then assumes the richly-clad form of Flora
as the next figure in the group. Venus, the personification
of April, stands in the centre of the picture gesturing
towards her attendant Graces. The picture is dulled and
darkened by surface dirt. It generally appears more
colourful in reproduction than 'in the flesh' as the
powerful lighting needed to photograph such a dark
image penetrates the dust and grime. The picture
remained at Castello until 1815, when it was transferred
to the Uffizi. It was in the Accademia for a spell
until 1919.

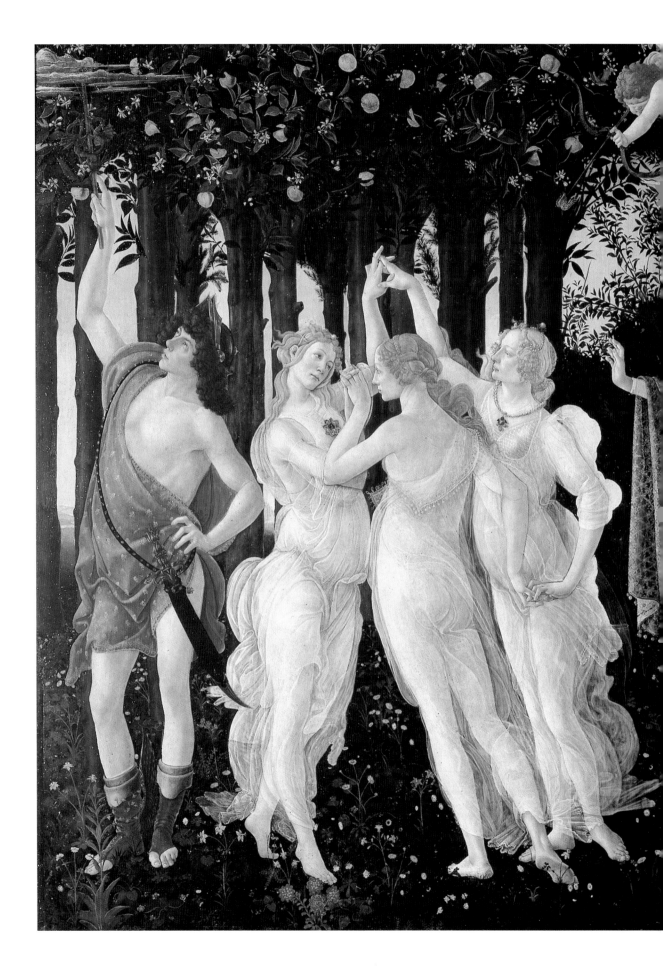

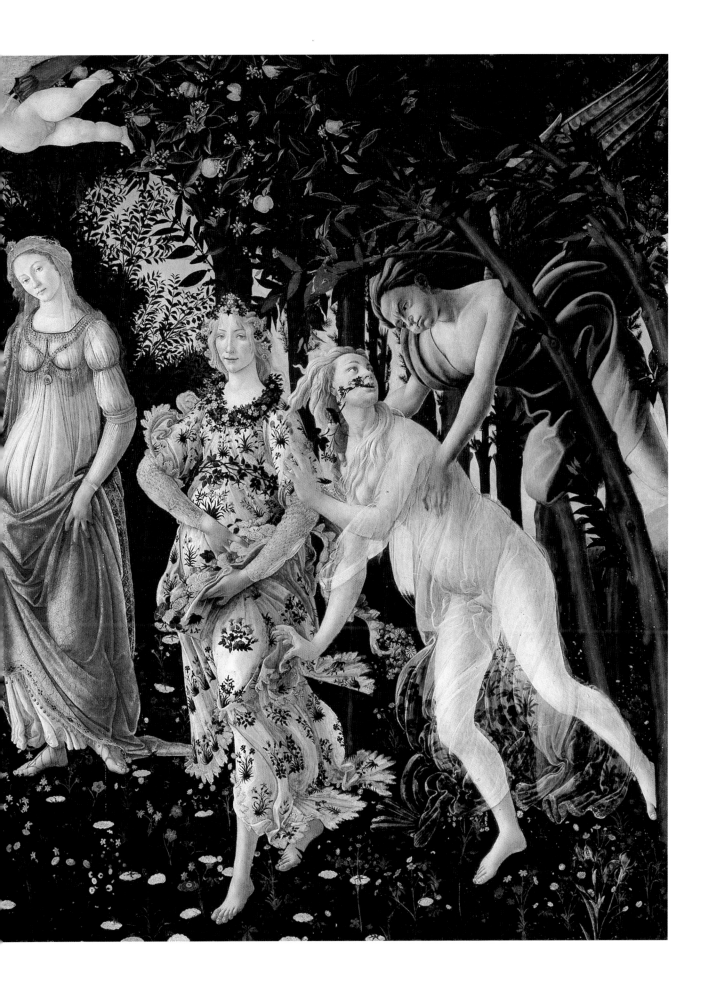

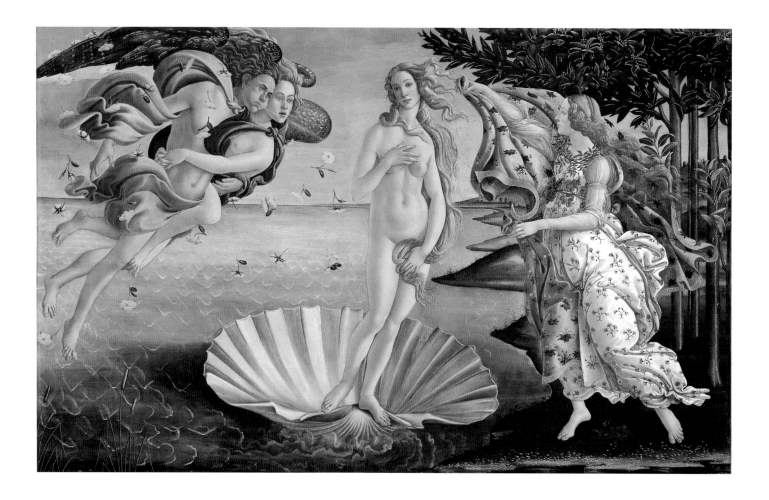

68 *The Birth of Venus*
FLORENCE, Galleria degli Uffizi.
Tempera on canvas 172.5 x 278.5 cm.
Probably transferred from panel; damage along a
horizontal join across the centre of the canvas has been
crudely retouched.

The Birth of Venus is Botticelli's best known and most
popular work, painted, like the *Primavera* (Plate 67), for
the Villa di Castello, though not as a pendant of the
earlier picture. The provenance of both paintings is the
same. The theme may be related to the Neo-Platonist
education of the young Lorenzo di Pierfrancesco de'
Medici for whom it was painted. Letters from the tutor
Marsilio Ficino to Lorenzo show that Venus was
imagined not as an erotic figure but as a symbol of
Humanitas, an image of beauty intended to inspire men's
most noble thoughts. The picture represents Venus's
spiritual birth: when Saturn castrated Heaven and threw
the testicles into the sea Venus was born from the foam.
The Birth of Venus was painted after Botticelli's return
from Rome, in the mid-1480s.

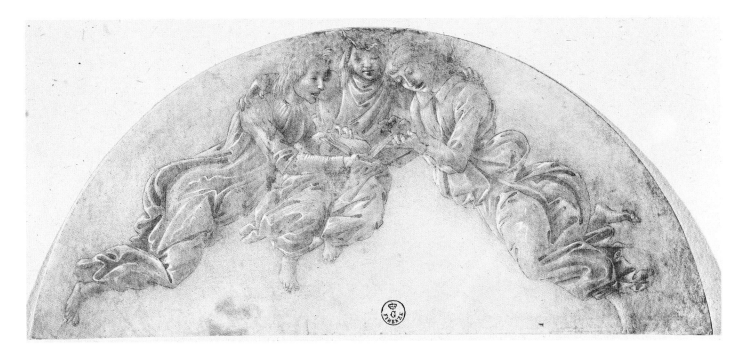

69 *Three Angels*
FLORENCE, Galleria degli Uffizi, Gabinetto dei
Disegni e Stampe.
Pen and ink on brown tinted paper, heightened with
white 10.2 x 23.5 cm.

Yashiro called this 'the finest example of the precision
and purity of the Quattrocento drawing'.

70 *Abundance*
LONDON, British Museum, Department of Prints and
Drawings. Pen and ink and wash over black chalk with
white heightening on tinted paper 31.7 x 25.3 cm.

Vasari recorded that he had in his collection several
drawings by Botticelli. When Horne saw the *Abundance* it
was set in what he believed to be one of Vasari's mounts,
but this has since disappeared. In its more recent history
it was sold by Rogers at Christie's, London in 1856 as by
Verrocchio, and subsequently owned by Morris, Moore,
Sir J. C. Robinson and Malcolm, from whom it passed to
the British Museum in 1895. The British Museum
cataloguers believe it to date from shortly after the
Primavera (Plate 67), while Horne and others place it after
Botticelli's visit to Rome.

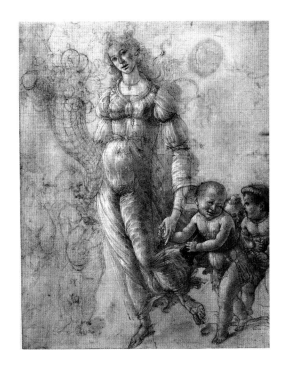

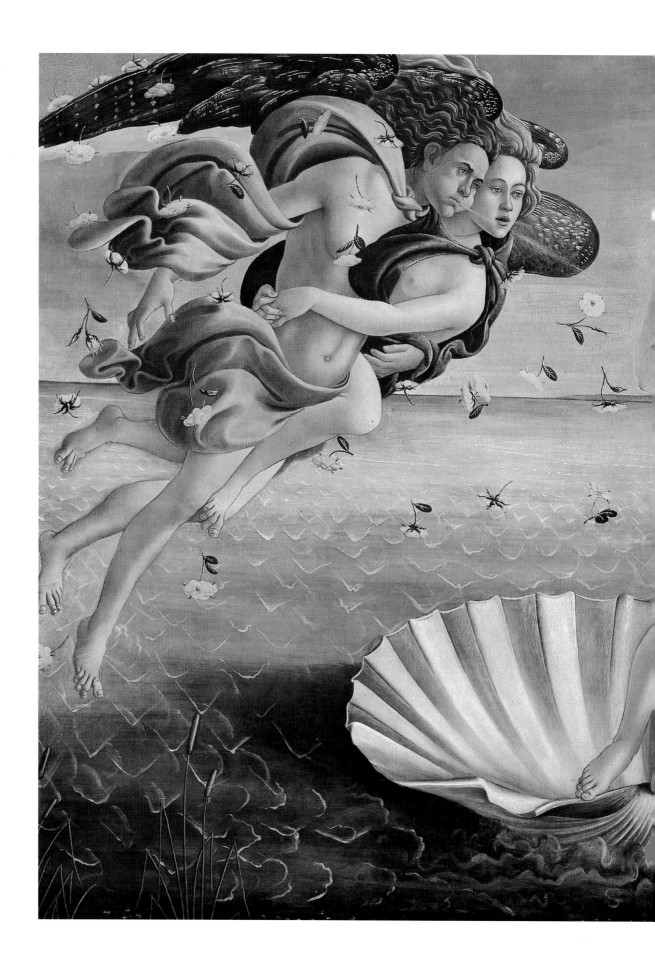

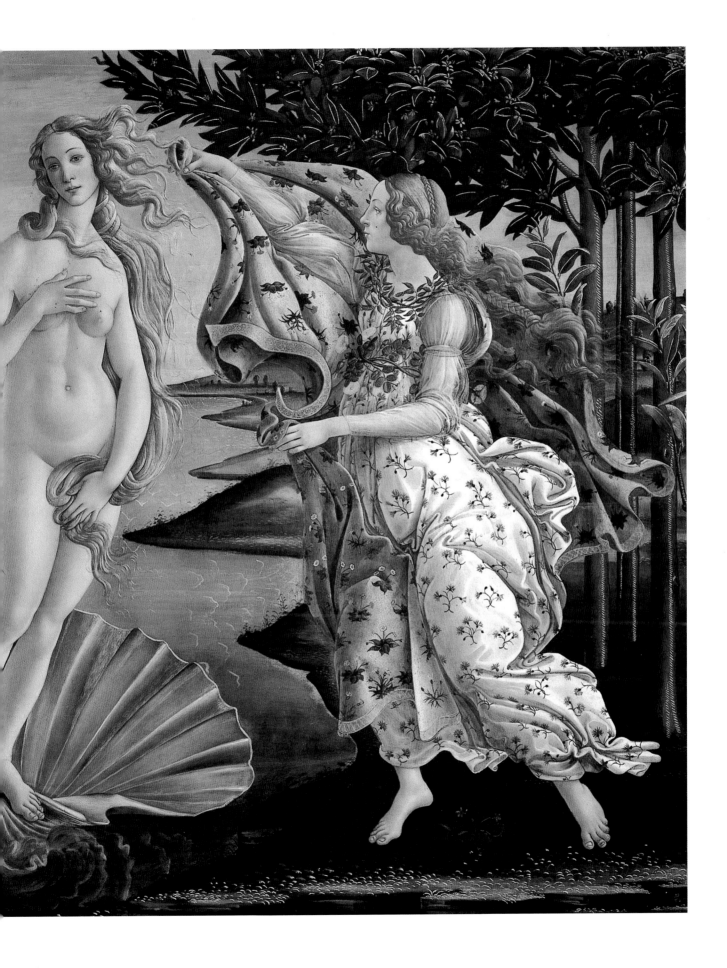

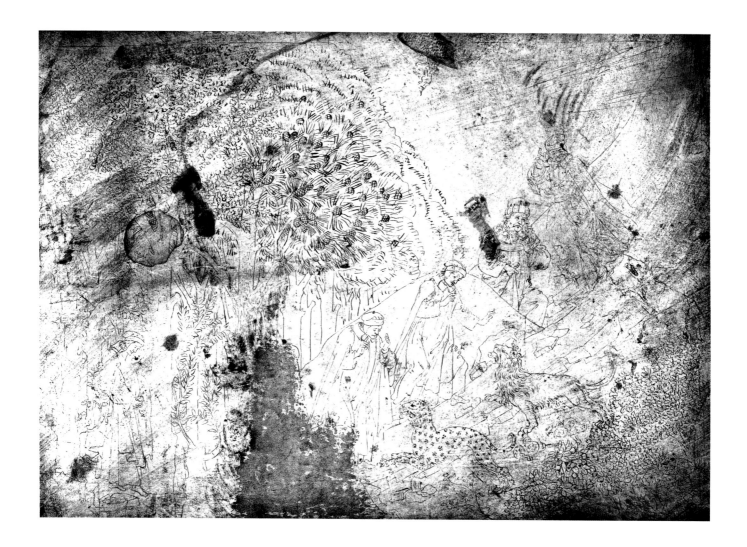

71 *La Divina Commedia, Inferno, Canto I*
VATICAN CITY, Biblioteca Apostolica Vaticana.
Silverpoint, pen and ink on vellum 32 x 47 cm.

Botticelli designed a number of illustrations for
Cristoforo Landino's 1481 edition of Dante's *La Divina
Commedia*. Nineteen of these were crudely engraved by
Baccio Baldini (cf. fig. 14), and we can only guess at the
quality of the original drawings as they are apparently all
lost. The magnificent series of drawings which survive in
Rome and Berlin is believed to be that which the
Anonimo Gaddiano recorded was made for Lorenzo di
Pierfrancesco de' Medici. Horne, noting that Lorenzo
fled from Florence in 1497, concluded that the drawings
must have been complete by that date, but Yashiro, calling

them 'the beautiful suicide of Botticelli's art', placed them
among the very latest of the artist's works. The Vatican
sheets (Cantos I and IX–XVI) of the *Inferno* were
acquired from Queen Christina's estate in 1690. It is not
known where they were earlier. *Inferno, Canto I* is the
beginning of *La Divina Commedia*. Dante, after wandering
lost in a forest, finds himself at the foot of a hill over
which the sun is just rising. Attempting to climb the hill,
he is driven back by a panther, a lion and a wolf. In fear
he turns back to the forest, but his course is changed, and
the whole story set in motion, by the appearance of
Virgil, who volunteers to be his guide. Beatrice hovers in
the sky above. The engraving of *Inferno, Canto I* in
Landino's *Divina Commedia* is close in design to
this drawing.

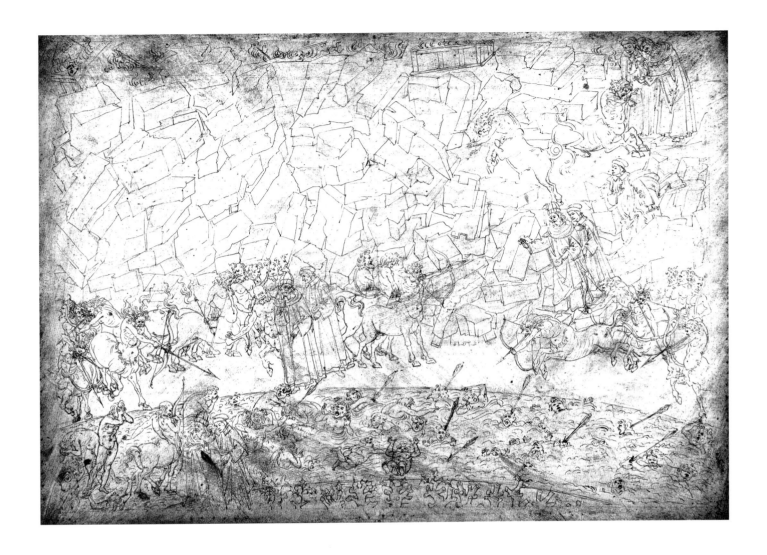

72 *La Divina Commedia, Inferno, Canto XII*
VATICAN CITY, Biblioteca Apostolica Vaticana.
Silverpoint, pen and ink on vellum 32 x 47 cm.

Descending a rocky path Dante and Virgil encounter the
Minotaur, whom Virgil orders aside so that they can pass.
They reach a ditch filled with blood in which flounder the
souls of the damned. Virgil persuades one of the herd of
centaurs, who are shooting arrows at the souls, to
accompany him and Dante as a guide. As in the majority
of the illustrations, the protagonists, Dante and Virgil,
appear more than once in the picture. The engraving of
the same canto in the Landino edition of *La Divina
Commedia* incorporates a portion of this design in reverse.

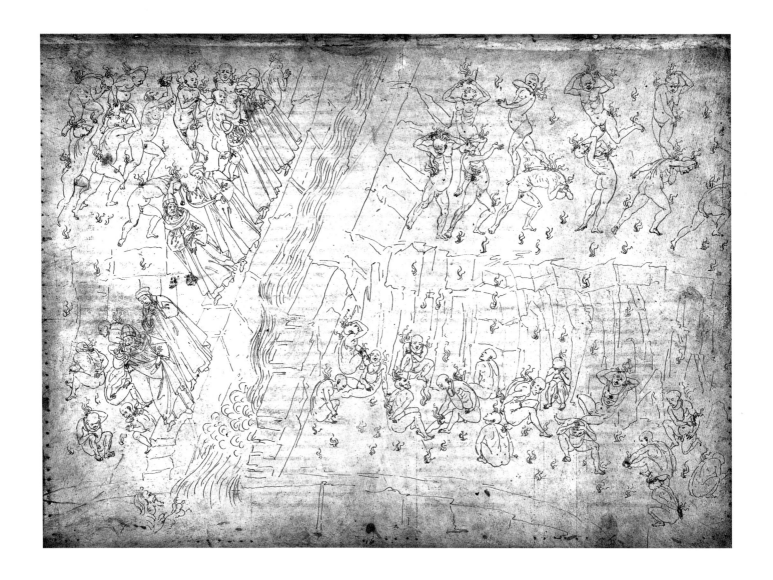

73 *La Divina Commedia, Inferno, Canto XVI*
VATICAN CITY, Biblioteca Apostolica Vaticana.
Silverpoint, pen and ink on vellum 32 x 47 cm.

Dante and Virgil come upon a band of sodomites doing
penance in a sea of sand and shower of flames. Virgil
tells Dante to unfasten the belt from his waist and lower it
into the ditch where the monster Geryon, in the lower left
corner, rises up and supports himself in front of them.
Usurers, each with a pouch round his neck, sit at the edge
of the precipice under a shower of flame. This scene, like
the preceding two illustrated here (Plates 71and 72), has a
counterpart in Landino's *Divina Commedia*, but the
composition in this case is quite different.

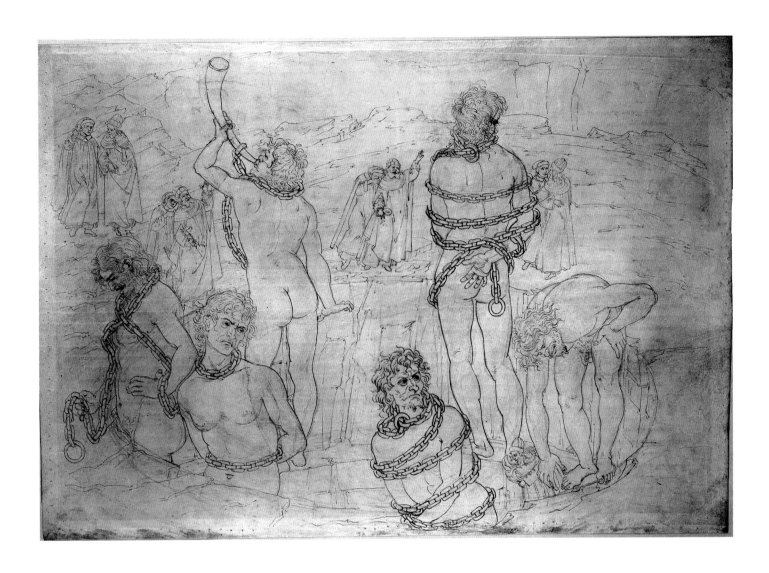

74 *La Divina Commedia, Inferno, Canto XXXI*
BERLIN, Kupferstichkabinett.
Silverpoint, pen and ink on vellum 32 x 47 cm.

The Kupferstichkabinett in West Berlin has illustrations
by Botticelli to the *Inferno*, Cantos VIII and XVII-XXXIV
and *Purgatorio*, Cantos I-VIII. In the Berlin
Kupferstichkabinett are *Purgatorio*, Cantos IX-XXXIII
and the complete *Paradiso*, Cantos I-XXXII. All the Berlin
drawings were acquired by the Duke of Hamilton from
the dealer Claudio Molino in Paris. He sold them to
Lippmann for the Berlin Museum in 1882. They were
divided between East and West Berlin after World War II.
In the illustration to Canto XXXI of the *Inferno* Dante
and Virgil find a group of chained giants standing near a
wall beyond which is the last circle of the Inferno. One of
the giants, Nimrod, blows a horn, and Antaeus on the
right lifts Dante and Virgil and places them inside the last
circle.

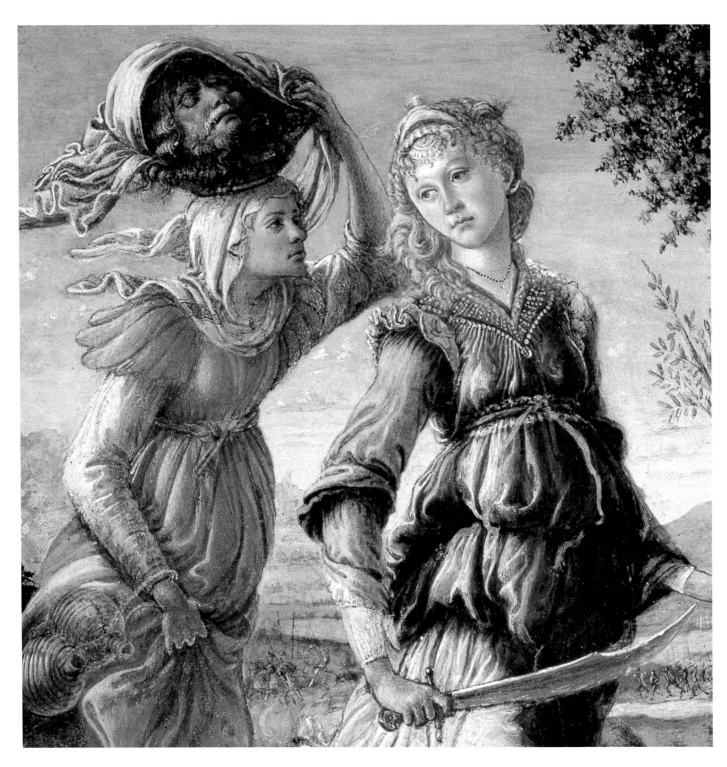

Detail of *The Return of Judith* (Plate 57)

BIBLIOGRAPHY

The giant monograph by Herbert P. Horne, Alessandro Filipepi, commonly called Sandro Botticelli (London 1908) is irreplaceable. It is painstakingly researched and quotes documents in full, including the relevant text of the Anonimo Gaddiano, originally written c. 1542–48, and both editions of Vasari's Life of Botticelli (1550 and 1568). Yukio Yashiro's Sandro Botticelli and the Florentine Renaissance (London 1929) is more passionately written and contains a useful chronology and extensive bibliography. For quick reference Roberto Salvini, Tutta la pittura del Botticelli, 2 vols. (Milan 1958) and The Complete Paintings of Botticelli, introduction by Michael Levey and with notes and catalogue by Gabriele Mandel (English edition, London 1970), are both easy to use. The most recent publications are L. D. and Helen S. Ettlinger, Botticelli (London 1976), Kenneth Clark, The Drawings by Sandro Botticelli for Dante's 'Divine Comedy' (London 1976) and a new monograph by Ronald Lightbown, Botticelli (London 1977). Of all the museum and gallery catalogues containing works by Botticelli, Martin Davies's National Gallery: The Earlier Italian Schools (2nd edition, London 1961) remains the most informative.

Rather than attempt to give a definitive bibliography which could cover several pages, I list here sources which have been quoted in my text and in general those books or articles which, in addition to the ones cited above, have proved most useful in the compilation of this book.

Francesco Albertini, *Memoriale di Molte Statue et Picture di Florentia* (Florence 1510) reprinted in *Gregg International Publishers' Five Early Guides to Rome and Florence* (Farnborough 1972).

Aldo Bertini, *Drawings by Botticelli* (New York 1968).

Francesco Bocchi, *Bellezze della Città di Firenze* (Florence 1591) and the Giovanni Cinelli edition of 1677.

P. Cannon-Brookes, 'Botticelli's "Pentecost", An Interpretation', *Apollo* (1962).

Julia Cartwright, *Sandro Botticelli* (London 1903).

J. A. Crowe and G. B. Cavalcaselle, *The History of Italian Painting* (Langton Douglas edition in English) (London 1911).

Kenneth Clark, *Another Part of the Wood* (London 1974).

C. Dempsey, 'Botticelli's Three Graces', *The Journal of the Warburg and Courtauld Institutes* (1971).

C. Dempsey, 'Mercurius Ver: The Sources of Botticelli's "Primavera" ', *The Journal of the Warburg and Courtauld Institutes* (1968).

L. D. Ettlinger, *The Sistine Chapel before Michelangelo* (Oxford 1965).

E. H. Gombrich, 'Apollonio di Giovanni', *The Journal of the Warburg and Courtauld Institutes* (1955).

E. H. Gombrich, 'Botticelli's Mythologies', *The Journal of the Warburg and Courtauld Institutes* (1945).

C. Grayson, *Leon Battista Alberti: On Painting and On Sculpture* (London 1972).

Martin Kemp, 'Botticelli's Glasgow "Annunciation": Patterns of Instability', *The Burlington Magazine* (1977).

Michael Levey, 'Botticelli and 19th century England', *The Journal of the Warburg and Courtauld Institutes* (1960).

Michael Levey, *Themes and Painters in the National Gallery Number 11: Botticelli* (London 1974).

F. Lippmann, *Drawings by Sandro Botticelli for Dante's 'Divina Commedia'* (London 1896).

M. Meiss, *The Great Age of Fresco* (London 1970).

W. and E. Paatz, *Die Kirchen von Florenz* (Frankfurt-am-Main 1955).

J. G. Phillips, *Early Florentine Designers and Engravers* (Cambridge, Massachusetts 1955).

H. Ruhemann, 'Technical Analysis of an Early Painting by Botticelli', *Studies in Conservation* (1955).

John A. Symonds, *Renaissance in Italy, The Fine Arts* (London 1877).

Agostino Taja, *Descrizione del Palazzo Apostolico Vaticano* (Rome 1750).

G. F. Waagen, *Works of Art and Artists in England* (London 1838).

H. Wölfflin, *Classic Art* (first published 1899; English edition, London 1952).

F. Zeri, *La Galleria Pallavicini in Roma* (Florence 1959).